## Praise for *You Are Amazing*

"*You Are Amazing* is a down-to-earth, practical, and fun guide to living a life based on intuitive guidance and being in touch with your Spirit. Written in their twenty-something, fresh, and uplifting voices, these daughters of the wonderful intuitive Sonia Choquette bring their legacy of inner guidance to a new generation. And they show us that ultimately, the path of intuition and guidance from the heart are the only ways that bring lasting fulfillment—so why not start early."

— CHRISTIANE NORTHRUP, M.D., *New York Times* best-selling author of *Goddesses Never Age*

"Sonia and Sabrina Choquette-Tully were raised to trust their vibes. In this carefree, high-spirited book, they share their many secrets. Join them on the road to happy, successful living."

— JULIA CAMERON, best-selling author of *The Artist's Way*

"This is a much-needed book for our younger generation who are now heading into uncertain times, given the current political climate. Written by two beautiful and down-to-earth young women, *You Are Amazing* is a practical guide for creating an empowered and authentic life. Through the use of colorful language, the ideas they share are very important for our time. I highly recommend this book."

— ANITA MOORJANI, *New York Times* best-selling author of *What If This Is Heaven?*

"It's time to be *amazing*—to trust your vibes, to be courageous, and to follow your joy! Sabrina and Sonia have written a spirited, fun, wise, and practical guide to show you how."

— ROBERT HOLDEN, best-selling author of *Authentic Success* and *Shift Happens!*

"A relatable and rich guide for living an amazing, intuitive, unlimited life. This is a must read for all millennials."

— REBECCA CAMPBELL, international best-selling author of
*Light Is the New Black* and *Rise Sister Rise*

"Sonia and Sabrina have written a must-read book for their generation. Their voices are authentic, bright, and real. Equal parts insightful and fun, this book should not be missed. The sooner you get on board with their message that following your intuition is essential to living a fabulous life, the better. They know what they're talking about! Truly magical."

— COLETTE BARON-REID, best-selling author
of *The Map* and *Uncharted*

"Sonia and Sabrina Choquette-Tully are real-life badasses who aren't afraid to speak their truth. Their whole entire existence has been an immersion with intuition, and who better to lead you toward self-acceptance, love, and confidence than these two? I believe in the sacred work that these ladies are sharing. As soon as you meet them you feel like you've just met two new best friends who ooze love from head to toe. They're hip, hot, and honest, with courage that will lovingly guide the next generation toward what can only be described as the light. Thank you, Sonia and Sabrina. The world needs your book now more than ever!"

—KYLE GRAY, best-selling author of *Raise Your Vibration*

"Sonia and Sabrina were crawling their talk before they could even walk it, and what they teach in *You Are Amazing* is as natural to them as the air they breathe. I've had the honor of witnessing these spirited young women share their gifts on stage over the span of many years, and now these pages create a compass and true transmission from their hearts and souls to millennials everywhere."

— NANCY LEVIN, author of *Worthy*

# YOU ARE AMAZING

# Hay House Titles of Related Interest

*YOU CAN HEAL YOUR LIFE*, the movie, starring Louise Hay & Friends
(available as a 1-DVD program and an expanded 2-DVD set)
Watch the trailer at: www.LouiseHayMovie.com

*THE SHIFT*, the movie,
starring Dr. Wayne W. Dyer
(available as a 1-DVD program and an expanded 2-DVD set)
Watch the trailer at: www.DyerMovie.com

*DAILY LOVE: Growing into Grace*,
by Mastin Kipp

*LET IT OUT: A Journey Through Journaling*,
by Katie Dalebout

*LIGHT IS THE NEW BLACK: A Guide to Answering Your Soul's Callings
and Working Your Light*, by Rebecca Campbell

*REVEAL: A Sacred Manual for Getting Spiritually Naked*,
by Meggan Watterson

*THE UNIVERSE HAS YOUR BACK: Transform Fear to Faith*,
by Gabrielle Bernstein

All of the above are available at your local bookstore,
or may be ordered by visiting:

Hay House USA: www.hayhouse.com®
Hay House Australia: www.hayhouse.com.au
Hay House UK: www.hayhouse.co.uk
Hay House South Africa: www.hayhouse.co.za
Hay House India: www.hayhouse.co.in

# SONIA + SABRINA CHOQUETTE-TULLY

# YOU ARE AMAZING

## A HELP-YOURSELF GUIDE FOR TRUSTING YOUR VIBES + RECLAIMING YOUR MAGIC

**HAY HOUSE, INC.**

Carlsbad, California • New York City
London • Sydney • Johannesburg
Vancouver • New Delhi

*Published and distributed in the United States by:* Hay House, Inc.: www
.hayhouse.com® • *Published and distributed in Australia by:* Hay House Australia Pty. Ltd.: www.hayhouse.com.au • *Published and distributed in the United
Kingdom by:* Hay House UK, Ltd.: www.hayhouse.co.uk • *Published and distributed in the Republic of South Africa by:* Hay House SA (Pty), Ltd.: www
.hayhouse.co.za • *Distributed in Canada by:* Raincoast Books: www.raincoast
.com • *Published in India by:* Hay House Publishers India: www.hayhouse.co.in

*Cover design:* Bloom Designs Company, bloomdesigns.co
*Interior design:* Riann Bender

### Library of Congress Cataloging-in-Publication Data

Names: Choquette-Tully, Sonia, 1988- author. | Choquette-Tully, Sabrina,
   1989- author.
Title: You are amazing : a help-yourself guide to trusting your vibes +
   reclaiming your magic / Sonia Choquette-Tully, Sabrina Choquette-Tully.
Description: 1st Edition. | Carlsbad, California : Hay House, Inc., 2017.
Identifiers: LCCN 2017000201 | ISBN 9781401952334 (paperback)
Subjects: LCSH: Self-actualization (Psychology) | Self-esteem. | Happiness. |
   BISAC: SELF-HELP / Personal Growth / Self-Esteem. | SELF-HELP / Spiritual.
   | SELF-HELP / Personal Growth / Happiness.
Classification: LCC BF637.S4 C4994 2017 | DDC 158--dc23 LC record avail-
able at https://lccn.loc.gov/2017000201

Tradepaper ISBN: 978-1-4019-5233-4

10 9 8 7 6 5 4 3 2 1
1st edition, May 2017

Printed in the United States of America

# CONTENTS

# HI, LET'S BE FRIENDS

Hi, you gorgeous human being. How are you? Feeling a little "eh" about life? Wondering if you'll ever figure things out? You're not alone. We wrote this book because we care about you. We know that sounds crazy. You're probably thinking to yourself, *How can these ladies care about me? They don't even know me.* But we *do* know you. We know you picked up a self-help book looking for something. And that looking, that willingness to pick up a book and read something that isn't just fluff or pop culture, that makes you *our people*. We love you for being someone who wants, on some level, to learn something new in order to build yourself an amazing, unbelievable, dope-ass life.

What if we told you that you possess an innate wisdom that—should you choose to listen to it—not only improves your life, but gives you confidence and inspiration, strengthens your relationships and your community, and gives back to the world? It might sound too good to be true, but it's not. Pinkie promise! It's living a life that is connected to your Spirit and your intuition.

Before you roll your eyes and think, *Ugh, I'm over this already*, please give us another minute of your time (err, a few minutes, depending on how quickly you read). We're not here with magical fixes. We're here to take back what being "spiritual" means. It isn't a bunch of mumbo jumbo that makes no sense in the real world.

We're talking about a new, grounded spirituality. And if words like *Spirit* and *intuition* throw you off, just substitute them for something that feels better. But don't get caught up in religious interpretation; think of it as the nonphysical part of you that is fundamentally *who you are* without all the BS.

Do we still have your attention? Awesome.

Now for introductions: we're Sonia and Sabrina Choquette-Tully, sisters and best friends. We grew up in a very unique way—we were raised in a family of intuitives. That doesn't mean that we're going to read your thoughts or that we're "special," but it does mean that we were taught that our sixth sense, or our intuition, should be the compass by which we live our lives. (If you're wondering how your intuition and your Spirit are related, your intuition is the voice of your Spirit, that part of you that knows and feels and listens to the stuff that's below the surface.)

You might be wondering how we're even qualified to write this. We have learned much of what we know from our mom, Sonia Choquette, a world-renowned best-selling author, intuitive, and pioneer in her field. She teaches people how to get out of their heads and back into their hearts, where they can tune in to their intuition and follow the flow of life. In short, she's a badass.

Growing up in our household, we have never known another way. We don't know what it's like to live from a place where we aren't connected to our true selves. Our classroom is our lives. From the womb to now, we would sit and listen to our mom do readings, or we'd go to workshops and play in the back of the room. We would talk about our "vibes" at the dinner table. We grew up in an incubator where we were taught that the heart is an intelligent organ and that the little voice in our heads that's a jerk is our ego, and it should be trained like an unruly pet. Most important, our intuition was nurtured and listened to *always*. When we would have problems, we were asked, "Well, what does your intuition say?" Bad vibes were something real and important. Our education is still ongoing—to this day, we travel the world and have helped thousands of people learn how to tune in to themselves. And we love it. We have the best job in the world.

But we're also just like you. We're young people in our 20s who have friends, party, love fashion and traveling and food, and are learning how to make sense of the world, to find our place. The difference is that with our intuition as our compass, we move through life with trust and confidence—even if we don't know where the road is leading. We still have moments where we wonder about what's next, but it allows us to look at life as an exciting adventure, where we can look at people through the lens of "me and you" instead of "me against you."

This book was born of the seeds of our struggles and triumphs, as we have worked to create the lives we really want to live. We wrote it as a love letter to our generation because as we've gotten older, we've noticed that many people don't seem to have these tools. We see the struggle, we know the struggle, because we're in it too. We see it with our friends and loved ones—people who feel disconnected, lost, not knowing what direction to go in, who don't know their own voice from the voices of everyone else. The problems that are unique to our generation aren't meant to leave us stuck and feeling hopeless, anxious, and lost. Because the space we're all trying to get to—the house, the perfect husband or wife, the money, the family, the fame—is all just backdrop really. The place we *actually* need to open to is the space within ourselves that really knows who we are—our gorgeous hearts.

The world is changing, and we need to adopt a new model for living—one with intuition directly at the helm, one where we can live life with a quiet confidence that comes from trusting our selves and our own voices, moment to moment. Tuning in to our intuition isn't difficult. It's the way that we're naturally designed to live. We all have gut feelings, those moments where we know what is right but get lost in a sea of confusion that isn't necessarily ours.

We're here to give you simple ways to tune *you* back in to *you*. These tools will empower you to get out of your own way so you can live the life you want. It's not a magical solution, but it is new ground from which you can operate. It's a great way to get your brain to shut the fuck up and get on board with what you want without a lot of drama. And the best part? Living a spirited, bright, shiny life not only makes life easier, it makes life more fun.

If we've piqued your interest, read on to hear stories of our misadventures, and those of our clients and friends, and the life lessons we use to navigate the world. Kick back, grab a drink or a snack, and if you're open, we'll help you to listen in, trust your vibes, and connect to your power, your Spirit.

Love,
Sonia + Sabrina

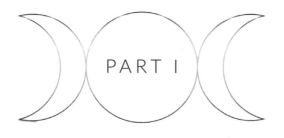

PART I

# WE'VE GOT SPIRIT, HOW ABOUT YOU?

CHAPTER 1

# THIS IS YOUR WAKE-UP CALL

## LET'S GET REAL

Do you ever have one of those quiet moments, maybe driving in your car, or walking down the street, where you have a moment of clarity and think to yourself, *What the hell am I doing with my life? Who am I?* We're a generation that craves authenticity; we're over all the BS we've been fed all these years. We're quick to call people on it too. Because we feel it. We want something real. We want something more. But we've been looking for it in all the wrong places—on social media, in shopping, on our smartphones, the idea being that one of these things must fill the void, right?

We've been thinking maybe we'll find relevancy, meaning, and connection if we succeed by other people's standards, whether that's the amount of likes on our Instagram feed or if we have the "perfect" job or outfit. Let us let you in on a little secret: you won't find what you're looking for in any of those places, and deep down, you know it too.

This thing you've been searching for, you've had all along. (Cue swelling music.) Really, though, we've grown up in such a noisy world that we've forgotten how to tune in and listen to ourselves. We inhabit a different world than our parents did when they were our age. We have been told that it's a cutthroat landscape, and only the strongest survive. Oh, and don't forget the death of the middle class, the disillusionment of the American dream, and soul-crushing student debt. The landscape has changed; everyone has a degree; everyone has done all the internships. The world we were promised doesn't exist anymore.

We're sure that we weren't the only kids whose well-intentioned parents encouraged an after-school regimen of SAT prep and extracurricular activities in order to get that "edge" to get into college. Downtime? Please. It is something to be scoffed at, a "waste of time." We have many friends who pride themselves on working till the wee hours of the morning just to wake up to do it all over again. Friends in the corporate world lament that if they want that raise or promotion, want to get noticed and viewed as an asset, they have to stay later than their boss who might work till ten. (Synergy, anyone?) Now, cram that 60-plus-hour work week (if you're really motivated) with any other combination—a social life, a love life, an hour at the gym, cooking, downtime (what is that?!), and poof! Your day/week/moment to yourself is gone.

The endless hamster wheel has left us exhausted, depleted, and numb. We've lost touch with our own true voice—the voice of our Spirit. We know this on some level already. With all the noise it's not surprising that we can't hear our deeper wisdom. We need to slow down, hop off the wheel of death, get quiet, start tuning in, and listen to our intuition.

Intuition resides in our heart space. We tend to forget that the heart is an intelligent organ. It is the first organ to develop, and it is how we measure life. The heart informs the rest of the body's early growth. The second organ to develop is the cochlea, or the inner ear. The cochlea picks up on vibrations, and as we continue to grow, our senses are informed by these primary organs. Our heart and our inner ear are our first intelligence. The heart and vibes are interconnected—the heart both emits and picks up on vibration. Our hearts have their own frequencies (i.e., a heartbeat) and are powerful. In fact, if measured by an EKG machine, the heart emits more electrical activity and even produces an electromagnetic field that is 5,000 times stronger than that of the brain.

We pick up on vibrations, or vibes, all the time, which is our intuition going to work, taking in information that is subconscious. Ever had a "woulda, coulda, shoulda" moment? One of those events where something didn't "feel" right and then something happened? You picked up on a vibration.

## BREAKING IT DOWN

What exactly do we mean when we talk about vibes, intuition, and Spirit? These terms may at first seem interchangeable, a woo-woo New Age mantra that feels vague and inaccessible. You might be saying to yourself, *Ladies, what the fuck are you talking about?* Great question. Before we go any further, let's make sure that we're all on the same page. First matter of business: intuition. Here are a few things that it is *not*:

- predicting the future
- reading people's thoughts
- talking to dead people
- using a crystal ball

Intuition is innate. It is not something that is outside of us. Intuition is the act of receiving information on an unconscious level. As human beings, we are receiving information all the time both consciously (the very words on this page of the book you're holding right now) and unconsciously (*Something about that person just makes me uncomfortable*).

Here's another way of thinking about it: your intuition is like your inner GPS. When it's awake and you can hear it, you can navigate life with ease. Having, building, and trusting your intuition means that wherever you go you'll feel safer, more grounded in yourself, trust your choices, and even be ready to change the world. Simply put, the solutions it provides are more effective, and you'll get to your intended result *faster*. It's the irony of our modern society: actually slowing down, breathing, getting grounded, working on yourself, and staying present will allow you to be more effective and move faster through the insanity we live in.

Intuition works in conjunction with two very powerful, often contradictory, partners. The challenge here is to begin unpacking the differences between your intuition, your emotions, and your mind. Once you understand how these are intertwined, you can tame the beast of your ego and harness the power of your intuition.

The mind is great; it helps us process all the information we are constantly bombarded with and categorizes it. It helps us make sense of the world in a logical, linear way. But our intellects are not the only way that we receive information, even though our society and schooling would tell us otherwise. Think of your intellect or ego (the voice of your intellect) as your superheady friend who always argues with you—the guy who always knows better. It is controlling, fact-obsessed, paints the world as black and white, and exists in terms of right and wrong. That said, since the ego is informed by the outside world, it can easily be confused (but would never admit it). It tricks us into listening to other people's opinions and gets trapped by its biggest nemesis, fear—the ego doesn't want to be made a fool of.

The ego is informed by the outside world, our experiences, and is in large part shaped by the traumas we've endured. Your brain has seen shit. It has been through broken relationships and uncomfortable, downright painful experiences. And all along it has been learning about the world from the moment your sweet little baby face opened your cute little baby eyes. From that moment your brain started learning and absorbing, taking in the world around you. And based on what you experienced, you might have learned to listen to everyone else *but* yourself.

Your ego would love for you to believe that its messages of fear and self-protection are coming from your intuition. It's sneaky like that. We form our ego as a way to protect ourselves, and it's great—if it's in check. Think of it as a dog that's constantly barking. You love your dog; you don't want to get rid of your dog, but you want to make sure that it's properly trained. But how do we tell the difference between the sneaky voice of our ego and that of our intuition? Ask yourself: How does it make you feel? Does it feel constrictive? Is it fearful? Or does it uplift? Is it creative and connecting or does it isolate you? Listening to your heart connects you, while listening to your ego disconnects you. It's as simple as that.

A more subtle distinction can be made between your emotions and your intuition. Emotions are vital—they communicate important information that we need to pay attention to. (For example, anger can communicate a need for boundaries.) Emotions can be misleading because we feel them so strongly in the body. But we must not confuse our emotional world with intuition. The simplest way to differentiate between the two is that emotions come and go, sort of like waves, a beach that is calm one moment and the next is a churning mess that might swallow any passersby in its chaos. But when you're out of the crashing waves of emotion, there's a deeper and generally much wiser voice. Your intuition isn't as dramatic as your emotion—it is grounded, steadfast, unwavering. It isn't going to be swayed by what you feel you want but instead is deeply rooted firmly in what you *need*.

Following your intuition is really just being able to listen to and trust your authentic self, your Spirit—your true voice. Not the voice of society, parents, friends, or ego. When you start to listen to your intuition, you can relax because you are no longer listening to your fears or other people's wishes. You intuitively know what you need, what is true, what works for you. You tune out your ego and start to relax and flow with life. Learning to listen to and trust your inner voice is absolutely vital to creating a magical, connected, and happy life. And we absolutely want to help you create a magical life.

That said, we are not advocating throwing your thoughtful brain out the window to follow only what you hope is your heart and just pray that everything works out. That works for some people (more power to ya!), but in most cases, that doesn't work all that great. The truth of the matter is that intuition works best when it works *with* our emotional and intellectual lives—they are complementary partners. BFFs, really. Being organized and informed (i.e., your intellect) not only allows us space to tune in to our intuition but also allows us to trust its guidance. We don't need to choose one over the other.

## LEARNING TO LOG OUT

When we talk to our friends and clients, they often ask, "How do I connect to my intuition?" Here is the first tool: be present. Easy, right? Not so much. In our lifetime, we have seen the birth of the Internet—a thunderous boom of technology that has infiltrated every aspect of our lives. Gone are the days of not being plugged in every single moment of every single day. (Have you checked your phone since you started reading this?) Sometimes we forget how plugged in we are. Here is a question: When you wake up in the morning, how long is it before you check your phone and inevitably your personal e-mail, work e-mail, Facebook, Instagram, Reddit, Tumblr, Snapchat, and whatever other social media outlets you choose to frequent? We're going to go out on a limb and guess that within an hour of greeting the day you've run the social media gauntlet at least once. And we get it. Our iPhones are the first things that greet us each the morning—literally the first thing that we touch. They are our best buddies in moments of boredom and our favorite fact-checkers at dinner. ("Oh my God! Did you see that video? Let me pull it up for you. . . . Just give me a second, I have to find it. . . .") Our smartphones have become our baby blankets and an extension of ourselves. We love them; we hate them; we can't live without them.

Have you ever watched a two-year-old panic when realizing she's dropped her blankie and can't find it? Have you ever observed yourself in the moment when you realize you've misplaced your phone? Similar reaction, no?

Recently there was a study published in *Science* magazine where they took a group of men and women and told them that they were going to be alone in a room for 15 minutes and their only task was to let their minds wander. Not that hard, right? But it was hard. People weren't able to do it. So the researchers did everything they could to make the task easier, even prepping the subjects with things to think about. Subjects who were at home while they completed this study admitted to cheating and picking up their phones at least once or twice. So the team kicked it up a notch: they brought the subjects into a lab and added some negative stimuli—a button that administered a small shock from a nine-volt battery. After receiving a "test shock," all the subjects said that they would pay a dollar or two *not* to get shocked again. The scientists then left the subjects alone for fifteen minutes, but this time there was that button, the one that would administer the shock that they just said they would pay to avoid. The million-dollar question: Would people prefer to be shocked instead of being alone with their thoughts? The answer to that question is *yes*. That's crazy, right?

In our society, the common thinking is that we need to be on top of our game 24/7, and if we choose to take a breath, to get grounded and connect, we might get left behind, replaced, or even worse, be "out of the loop." Taking time for our own thoughts? Who ever heard of such a thing?

Recently we met a friend of ours, Emily, at a Chicago café on a sunny summer afternoon. Emily arrived late, her hair in a messy bun and a Bluetooth headset attached to her ear. The bags under her eyes were strikingly purple. Every time one of us would try to begin a conversation with her, Emily's phone would ring and she would be taken out of the conversation. Working as a real estate broker, she could never relax, choosing instead to keep her phone on her at all times. Her fear of missing a sale or a client in need had created a person who was completely unavailable to the rest of the world around her.

"Are you happy with your work?" Sonia asked, hoping to at least dive a little deeper.

"Happy?! No, Sonia, I'm working. I'm not happy!" With that, her phone rang again, but this time the person on the other end of the phone was her boss. He was angry with Emily because she had not only shown up late to a client meeting but also had been on the phone with another client the entire time and had lost the listing. It was a half-million-dollar commission check lost. Emily was devastated.

The shock of the phone call sent her into rage, which quickly turned to despair. "All I ever do is work. It's literally *all* I do. I don't even see my friends anymore. I don't even feel like I should be here now."

It was obvious that Emily was lost without any idea why. She was doing everything her intellect had told her to do, but instead of succeeding, she was stuck disappointing everyone and failing across the board. Before we had even ordered lunch, she slammed a $20 bill on the table and was out the door, back on her cell phone.

Emily is a perfect example of how many people are unable to feel their inner instincts and connect to their heart space.

## PUMP THE BRAKES ON BUSY

Busy is better, whether it's productive or not—that's the American way. We have been supplied with every which way to increase productivity. No matter what, there's an app for that. Yet all this interconnectedness has left us feeling disconnected. We update our profiles to reflect what kind of life we're living. We Instagram our meals and take selfies everywhere, and it disconnects us from the present. By capturing the moment, we are snatched away from the *actual* moment.

Spirit is a subtle voice; it's not going to be able to compete with your cell phone, computer, iPad, or the news. In order to hear your Spirit you have to stop and listen. If you're so pushed up against the wall that you have no moment to check in with yourself, when are you supposed to be able to get any sort of guidance? The truth is you won't.

We are rarely encouraged to take a moment and check in with ourselves in present time. Take a moment; do it right now. Were you able to take a moment and be here? We spend valuable energy reliving the past and rehearsing the future. But the tricky thing is that we are only able to connect to our hearts in the "right now," so learning to get present is the first step.

Notice what takes you out of the present moment. What is drawing your energy? Are you reliving conversations? Rehearsing future conversations that may or may not ever take place? Are you worrying about the future? Or reliving the past? Or going through your to-do list? Are you exhausted? Are you trying to control someone else? These are all common vicious cycles that can keep you out of the present. It's easy to believe that if we get all the things on our list done then we will *finally* be happy, be peaceful, and feel okay. But the to-do list will never end. It's a mind game in which we set up constant obstacles between ourselves and our happiness. In our world that encourages us to constantly be on the go, we need to learn how to take a moment to pause and check in with ourselves.

Learning to be present is an ongoing process. We're not going to ask you to sit down cross-legged on the floor, close your eyes, and turn off your brain. Take it from us, we've tried; it doesn't work (although we do recommend the application Headspace as a good meditation training ground). However, learning to get present doesn't have to be a struggle, nor does it have to involve sitting anywhere, unless that floats your boat. So, how do you do it? First, decide that you *can* do it. No one drops into instant quiet, so begin at the beginning. We all have moments of presence all the time, but we don't notice them. In the car with your friends with the windows down in the summertime, singing at the top of your lungs? That's being present. Dancing your heart out? That's being present. Taking the time to smell a flower? Being present. Cooking an exciting new recipe? Being present. It's the act of quieting your mind and being in the moment. There are a million ways to practice being present, but they aren't something that you think yourself into. We were taught to sing and dance ourselves silly for ten minutes as a way to get present, and it's still, for us, the best and quickest way to get quiet.

Moments where you're joyful and feeling fully alive are all moments that you've been completely present. The hallmark of presence is that it's quiet up there—gloriously, awesomely quiet, if only for a moment. Within that small moment you experience a shift—now you're listening. When you're listening, you're in a receiving mode, and this is invaluable because it will allow you to listen to your own wisdom and vibes. When you start getting present, the best and easiest way is to simply pay attention. Even if you're sitting in traffic, take a moment, 60 seconds, and feel the seat beneath you, or the steering wheel. That's how you begin to train the mind.

### Sabrina's Apple Detox

*Last year I took an unintentional three-day sabbatical from my electronic life.*

*I say* unintentional *because I wasn't trying to do a technology detox.*

*Instead, both my cell phone and computer died at the same time. I dropped my broken electronic babies off at the Apple store to be fixed and didn't know what to do with my hands. I sat in the car and fidgeted with the radio for a while.* How did people LIVE before the invention of Spotify? Wait, I don't even know where I am. *I was only blocks from my apartment, but I had never actually paid attention to where I was. Usually, my Google Maps got me home. I was lost and bored. What should I do with myself?*

*Leading up to this technology meltdown I had been burning the candle at both ends, working too hard and not sleeping enough. I was saying yes to work and had not only a full schedule of clients but also a waiting list of ten more to be mentored. Each day I felt frustrated that I wasn't accomplishing enough, as though I was failing to show up for my own life.*

*Those first days without my electronics were anxious. A pressing feeling that I was missing something important loomed over me. I decided to go for a hike in the canyon outside my house, but the feeling that I had forgotten something plagued me. At first I was distracted, convinced that I was going to miss something important, running circles of worry in my head. I had convinced myself that I couldn't step back even for a moment. I was a psychic junkie who needed* to absorb every hit, and I couldn't relax. Despite counseling people out of the dangerous sea of overcommitment and distraction, I now found myself in deep waters.

I consciously pushed past this feeling, and slowly it started to lift. I realized—for the first time, although I had hiked this canyon many times before, regularly in fact—that there were small yellow flowers that lined each side of the trail. I had never even noticed them. How was that possible?

It's amazing how much I had been able to tune out. I went into the world to hike, but instead of listening to the sound of my footsteps or my own breath, I always had earbuds hooked up to my head. No wonder I was so disconnected! I hadn't slowed down to check in with myself in months.

Three days later, I picked up my revived laptop and iPhone from the Apple store. My screens lit up, and once again I was back online. The best part: instead of finding anything important, I found absolutely nothing. No e-mails looking for me or upset clients. No bad news. Instead, I opened my computer life to find nothing but junk.

This is how the universe works. I needed to be shaken out of my own electronic daze to realize that I needed sleep and relaxation. Our energy is being stolen right from under our noses! It's time to take it back and take responsibility for where it is going.

---

Your environment can either bring you closer to being able to hear your Spirit, or further away. Without judgment, and with compassion, take a good, honest look at your life. How much time do you spend watching television? How much time do you spend on the phone? Surfing the Internet? Listening to the news? Now ask yourself, *How much time do I spend focusing my attention inward?* Technology can be like a good or bad relationship. We're suggesting that, like a wonderful, crazy, fun friend, you keep it around but don't let it run your life. Be smart about understanding what does and doesn't support you. If you want to cut out the bullshit and hear your own heart, putting some protective measures in place is the first step. The truth of the matter is that you don't need a lot of time to reconnect to your authentic self—just a few minutes a day will go a long way.

Now, more than ever, we need to take time to get quiet and tune in to our intuition. We are a generation that is bombarded with information, and, as a result, there is a lot of fear and panic. If we don't get grounded and tune in to Spirit, it's incredibly easy to get caught up in the tidal wave of bad news and fearmongering and lose sight of what we want and what we can create. Beyond that, since we have gotten the short end of the stick in terms of the economy, jobs, and the overall social climate, it's easy to keep doing what we feel like we *should* be doing instead of what we *want* to be doing. After graduating from college, we have seen many of our friends get stuck in jobs that they despise, convinced that their choices are limited. So they remain trapped. A close friend recently lamented: "No matter what, everything is going to be miserable anyway, so I just have to suck it up." How depressing! And untrue. This is a woeful example of a fearful ego running the show. For her, nothing will shift because she won't allow herself to imagine anything else.

We have been told over and over again that we're stuck, but it's just not true. We need to remember who we are—beautiful, wise Spirits—what we want, and what we need without all the din around us telling us otherwise. As a generation, we're craving something different. We want authenticity. There has been a shift toward cynicism, but that cynicism has a hidden purpose. It's pointing out what's no longer working. If instead we connect to our hearts and allow our intuition to lead, we get creative and find that we have endless possibilities. In reconnecting with our intuition, we take back our power and choose to create a life that we want. We escape the "struggle" and reconnect to our creativity, our imagination, and most of all our happiness.

Intuition is innate within all of us, and it's not difficult to tune in to it. Our egos would like us to believe otherwise, but if we choose to start taking care of ourselves, our inner guidance is just a quiet moment and a breath away. Decide that for the next week, you're going to give yourself just a few minutes a day to stop whatever you're doing and just be. If the mental marathon of what needs to be done barges in, acknowledge it, remind yourself it's not an emergency, and take ten deep breaths. Go for a walk around the block. Take the pressure off and allow yourself to start to feel and hear the voice of your Spirit.

## HELP YOURSELF

- Slow down. Life is not a race to the finish line.

- Disconnect from your gadgets for five minutes a day. Silence the phone, put away the laptop, turn off the TV, and just be quiet.

- Get back into your body. Sing, dance, shout, play, run. Do anything physical that will bring you back to your body. It will center you.

- Breathe deeply.

- Eat well. Taking care of your body makes you feel better, which allows you to be present!

# CHAPTER 2

# WHO ARE YOU?

## INTUITION IS A CHOICE

One sunny Saturday at the park, we asked our goddaughter Allie, who was four years old at the time, where her Spirit lived. She pointed to her heart and proudly stated, "Here." It was freaking adorable and she was absolutely correct.

Human beings instinctively point to their hearts when asked where their Spirits live. Your heart is your main source of power. Who are you? What do you love? Does your heart have a voice, or is it stuck, buried under the daily grind? We make conscious choices every day. Most of the time we choose to ignore what speaks to our hearts and fool ourselves into believing that we're making "practical" or "adult" decisions, while in reality, we are setting ourselves up for resentment. We ignore our intuition and file its subtle voice into a category of "maybe later." We decide maybe next year, maybe next lifetime, for that matter, we'll get around to creating the life we really want to live.

When we first leave the safety of school and go into the big, wide world, we have dreams—maybe it's traveling the world or finding a job that we're passionate about. Yet we get stuck in "practical loops," and although they might satisfy us on a basic level, those promptings of our hearts never leave. We just get more skilled at ignoring them until we have a midlife crisis and ask, "What in the world have I done with my life? Why did I always believe that my happiness would arrive later?"

In choosing to tune inward, you become your own authority and get out of the chaos other people's energy and opinions. Listening to your intuition allows you to cut through a lot of bullshit and create a life that you want, without a lot of drama.

Slow down and tune in. Get back in touch with what you love, who you are, what you need, and where you want to go—all of the essentials for living a fulfilled life.

## THE HEAD VS. THE HEART

Your heart knows what it loves. Your heart knows what makes it sing and dance and laugh and cry. It connects to life and is open, loving, forgiving, and accepting. Your heart is strong and courageous, and it lifts other people up and brings goodness to the world. Your head, on the other hand, judges. Your head tells you you're not safe. Your head argues against your feelings. And it is feelings, gut, in-the-body feelings, that make us truly human.

Living a Spirit-driven life is living a full and fabulous life. We have seen people break outside of their comfort zones and create truly magnificent shifts away from their own limitations and into new lives that are incredible. The common thread for each of these people was a willingness to do something new. A two-feet-in approach, a throw-caution-to-the-wind attitude, and even a dash of whimsy.

What we're suggesting is to forget about what you *think* you want, and instead focus on what it is you want your life to *feel* like. Too often we see people disconnect from their hearts, trying desperately and utterly failing at creating anything fulfilling at all. Now, herein lies the problem. In order to create a full, lush, and—dare we say it—fantastic life, you have to authentically connect to your heart. Have you ever said to yourself, *I really want that. If I just get [fill in the blank here—the job, the boyfriend, the house, the vacation], I think I'll be happy,* but when you succeed, what you thought you wanted isn't right at all? You might have even bent over backward, spent all your money, or made yourself crazy because your mind was hell-bent on getting it. The mind is tricky because it can convince you that in the future, you'll feel happy if you just power through and get there (wherever "there" is). So you spend YEARS putting your feelings aside, disconnecting from your heart, and not listening to your intuition.

When we get too heady, we inevitably build a wall between our experiences and ourselves. When we instead live by how we want our life to *feel* we allow ourselves to get out of our heads and get into life. With our intuition at the reins, we are open to infinite possibilities, creative problem solving, and flexibility. We call this being "hungry for _____." When we start to access our creative self, we see the connections. We don't think—we feel and react instantly. We allow ourselves to bypass the brain and fear-driven ego and connect to the creative self—the problem solver.

Believing in the power of your own heart is the first step. The second is to begin empowering yourself to trust what it tells you is important. Even if it doesn't make sense to the logical mind, your heart isn't an asshole trying to slow you down. Instead, your heart is your true nature. When feeling connected to your life is your motivation, the rest of the ducks fall into a row. What we've seen mirrored back to us over and over again, with clients, and even in our own family, is that it doesn't actually matter what things look like. Be mindful of making decisions in life because of how others will see those choices. Instead, recalibrate yourself back to your own heart. Then make choices from the place of your heart and how it feels, and from there you can build a truly authentic and real life.

## GETTIN' IN TOUCH WITH YOUR INNER WEIRDO

Look, we're not going to kid you. This isn't unicorns, rainbows, sunshine, and everyone sitting in a circle singing "Kumbaya." Life is tough, people's opinions are loud, and it's not always easy to do what honors you, especially if you've been listening to the proverbial peanut gallery your whole life. Living an intuitive life isn't for the faint of heart. Sometimes, it means making choices that go against the grain, forcing yourself to be temporarily uncomfortable. Living an authentic life takes courage—choosing to act rightly in the face of popular opinion, opposition, or discouragement. Consider this: the word *courage* comes from the French word *coeur*, or *heart*. Sometimes you have to walk through the fire, but honoring yourself, your Spirit, and your intuition is always worth it.

Our friend Hannah is on the front lines of this war. She is a beautiful, talented, wonderful lady who wants to break into the music industry. Driven and hardworking, she has been trying to make this happen since graduating college back 2014. She's close with her parents, who adore her, but they don't see the value in her dream. They would rather she get a typical nine-to-five job, launch a more "responsible" career.

At her birthday party, Hannah still felt torn between following her dreams and listening to her parents' advice to enter corporate America. She had to admit that they had a point—they had helped her pay for college, and here she was, taking odd jobs in the music industry just to support herself. Hannah worked festivals and did everything from work the box office to vend food. But she wasn't giving up yet. Dinner wound down, and it came time to open presents. The first gift was a loud pair of pants for "festival season" and a lace top. She was overjoyed. "Mom, these are perfect!" Her mom responded with a somewhat disapproving look. "Next year, I hope to be buying you a pantsuit and work pumps instead of festival gear." It was such a tiny comment, but

Hannah felt derailed. After dinner, we sat in the car and she lamented that she enjoyed the passion, hard work, and adventure of the music industry—an office job sounded like death. Her path remains unclear as her heart and "convention" battle it out.

Tuning in to your heart can give you the courage to follow your passion. Just as crucial, it can shine a bright light on what brings you happiness, as well as what diminishes your Spirit. This is why it takes a certain amount of bravery to pause, really listen to yourself, and tackle the changes that are necessary for growth. But it also might mean turning away from mainstream culture. It might mean abandoning normalcy and embracing being an individual.

It takes balls to begin to take action in your life toward creating a life that's truly spectacular. It might mean that you need to branch out into the world and come across as a little weird. Because the definition of *weird* is "something supernatural; unearthly." So bring it on, we say! Let's embrace being courageous, heart-driven weirdos.

---

## Sabrina Channels Beyoncé

*John works as a celebrity stylist in Los Angeles and travels with some of the biggest stars in the world. He is incredibly successful and vibrant and has, by all accounts, built himself a gorgeous life at 30. But instead of feeling centered, he has been constantly trying to "keep up" with the world around him. He feels overspent and drained, drinking coffee to wake up and wine to fall asleep. John can't relax, especially in situations where a lot is being asked of him.*

*I sat with him at Cecconi's in Los Angeles for a glass of rosé when all his self-animosity came tumbling out. His coping mechanisms were burning him out, and he was tired,* bloated, and unhappy. "Can you slow down with me just for a second?" I asked, putting my hand on his as he started to tear up.

"I just want to know why, given everything I'm doing, and how hard I'm working, I'm still miserable. There is so much I want to change about myself, and I just don't even know where to begin."

When John slowed down, the pressure cooker of his life felt unmanageable.

"I know exactly how you feel," I comforted him, and now the two of us were crying in the bougiest restaurant in West Hollywood. I got it—I had put so much emphasis on where I wasn't succeeding in my own life that I knew the feeling of just never fully keeping up. "It's a bitch for my self-esteem! And everyone just thinks I have it all together, but inside I'm struggling too."

Instead of focusing on where we were succeeding, our attention was squarely on where we weren't enough. And it was true, John needed to stop drinking so heavily and get himself more present, but the truth was he didn't even have the self-confidence to create changes in his life. I see this often. We get so identified with our wounds and enmeshed in our emotions that we lose touch with our Spirit and our light. John and I spent the rest of the evening getting grounded around what we needed to do to take better care of ourselves.

We decided that Beyoncé's "Grown Woman" would be our theme song as we navigated success, failure, love, loss, and even hangovers. In it, she honors her freedom and the power to be her awesome self.

*We were learning what it meant to be adults in the world, but if we centered ourselves on what we loved about each other and put ourselves first, growing up just didn't feel so heavy. It could even feel empowering to find something we wanted to change and grow.*

---

## DON'T WE ALL LIKE TO THINK OUR SHIT DON'T STINK

Being real with ourselves, our bullshit, our messiness, is a source of empowerment. We've been taught to pretend we've "got it," as if messing up and copping to it should be a source of shame. But in reality, if you're honest with yourself and where you need to grow, it's not a shame fest. It's not surprising that we repeat the same shit over and over again—when it happens *yet again*, it makes us want to pull our hair out. But if we shift our perspective and think, *What am I contributing to this equation?* we step out of the matrix.

If we're able to look at our weak spots head on, we shift out of *Groundhog Day*. Getting the life we want isn't magical thinking. We've got to roll up our sleeves and unclog that shit. This includes looking at ourselves and our shit from a neutral place. Our shit doesn't make us good or bad—it's just learned patterns, different tools that we've learned to cope with life. Some work, some don't.

We've been trained to think of this as being vulnerable, and we've grown up in a culture that doesn't allow us to ask for help. Admitting any vulnerability might feel like defeat. It's not. It's your best tool to remove yourself from the drama shit storm that seems to repeat over and over again. Looking at our own self-perpetuated problems can be hard, but it's like the skeleton in the closet. It's a lot scarier in your imagination than in real life. In real life, after you turn on the closet light, you think, *Who put this stupid plastic skeleton in here?*

Our shit is usually just our reactionary response, our triggers. It's our autopilot to deal with uncomfortable or hard things. But most times, they are just patterns. Patterns are our most primitive tools for survival that we learned subconsciously growing up. That skeleton is just a pattern, and that makes it feel a lot less scary. If we don't look at our patterns and learn from them, we get caught in the same loop and repeat the same mistakes over and over again. That's a lot scarier than the skeleton in your closet.

When we tune in to our intuition, we tap into our deeper wisdom. That wise part of us isn't just here to inflate our egos and tell us we're perfect and that everyone else is the problem. Its true purpose is to help us grow and evolve on a soul level. That means shining a light in those not-so-nice places.

Patterns are wonderfully adaptive in the sense that they allow you to go into autopilot in order to feel protected. However, they are also a great way to stop you from connecting to your authentic self. The defensive patterns that are supposed to keep you safe usually keep you disconnected from people. What are the patterns that keep you from being your authentic self?

Patterns like to disguise themselves as your authentic self. They make you parade around and go, "Well, that's just who I am, so you just need to deal with it." Though there may be some truth to this, most of it is just posturing that allows you to escape culpability. Hidden in that statement is the fear of change. It's scary to address patterns. But, like what is said to an addict, admitting that you have a problem is the first step.

---

## It's Not You, It's Me

*Claire and Ryan had been dating for more than a year. She was very much in love with Ryan, but as time wore on, her gilded boyfriend who "could do no wrong" was starting to show some of his unpleasant patterns. She did not know what to do. Claire was very self-aware. She had been raised in an environment where her family talked about how they felt, processed issues until they were resolved, and constantly worked on communication. However, her boyfriend's family did not talk about emotions, and he didn't know how to engage in conversations where she was trying to resolve their emotional issues. Ryan tried desperately to conform to her needs, but it seemed like he wasn't getting it fast enough.*

*She called me, frustrated: "Sonia, I tell him what's wrong, what I want him to do in order to fix it. I give him clear instructions and try my best not to hold on to our fights. But it almost seems like he doesn't want to get it. Maybe we're just two different people and this isn't going to work in the long run."*

*My first reaction was to laugh. I too come from a family that processes, talks (sometimes in circles), and loves deeply. I could relate to the difficulties of being in a relationship with someone who was raised very differently from myself. The thing that stuck out most to me was that she assumed this situation was Ryan's problem to fix, not her own.*

*She was trying so hard, explaining exactly what was wrong, but she had a pattern of impatience. She wanted it fixed, and she wanted it fixed now. Claire had unrealistic expectations of her boyfriend. He wasn't going to change overnight. That would take time. And Claire's problem of impatience wasn't only limited to her boyfriend. It was apparent in every project she undertook. She wanted to get to the finish line without doing any of the work. I could see it permeating the nooks and crannies. Claire was ambitious; she wanted to conquer the world . . . from her couch.*

*She wanted to start up a business but didn't know where to begin. She put up a website but didn't understand why people just didn't "come." She kept talking and talking until I gently interrupted her.*

*"Would you consider yourself a patient person?"*

*Her response was overwhelming and strong. "Of course!" she snapped. "I am very patient." But even her response was impatient. She clearly did not want to hear anything contrary to what she believed to be true. Her boyfriend, her business, nothing was her problem. They were other people's problems—people who did not know how to get things done quickly like she did. And that was the problem. I broke it down simply and directly. "Claire, you are putting in the groundwork and then walking away as if that's enough. Honestly, you need to tend your gardens." At this, she was quite defensive, citing that I just didn't understand. We got off the phone, and I felt exhausted and a little worried that she had taken offense at my suggestions.*

*A few days later, an e-mail from Claire surfaced in my inbox. She explained that she had been out to dinner with Ryan when they started having an argument that they had had a million times before. She could tell that he was trying extremely hard to not go into his comfort zone of shutting down, struggling to be open about what was going on. Still, she found herself getting more and more angry. She recognized his efforts but felt she couldn't stop the snowballing effect of her fury. All of a sudden, she realized that she was being incredibly impatient. Instead of appreciating his efforts, she wanted him to hurry up. And that's when the patience seed that I had planted started to flower.*

*It was her "aha" moment. Claire realized that this pattern was the culprit of her issues. She didn't want to wait. She told me that she'd lain awake in bed that night detailing all the ways that her impatience had cost her opportunities, spoiled relationships, and kept her small. "Patience feels like an overrated virtue," she wrote. "My parents were always movers and shakers. They didn't have time to wait around to see. They wanted things done right away. And I adopted that mentality. I honestly don't even know where to begin."*

*I thought we should start with basics. I encouraged her to examine what triggered her impatience. In learning about patterns, we need to learn where they come from in order to break the hold that they have on us.*

---

So how can you tell if a certain behavior is a pattern? It is usually the well-worn, comfortable path, even though it typically drops you off deep in the woods.

- Pay attention when you're fighting or doing things that you "always do."

  For example, if you have a pattern of avoidance, write down how avoiding the problem played out. Maybe you became worried about what the other person would think or how they would react. If you withheld information, did that work out to your advantage? Try and start from the beginning. An example of this would be your roommate not putting away her dishes. A factor map could look like this: you noticed that your roommate didn't put away her dishes, it irritated you, you complained to your friend, you wanted to say something to your roommate but didn't want to be a nag, your roommate left dishes out again, you made passive-aggressive comments, she reacted defensively, and the two of you fought.

- What is the common factor?

Once you have found your pattern, list at least five instances of it. Taking the pattern of avoidance as an example, look at when else that has cropped up into your life. Maybe it was when you had to deliver bad news or turn down an offer. Once you have a sample of different situations where the same problem came up, you can find the common factor or trigger. After you have made your list and found most of your triggers, find what the common thread is across the incidents.

- Home in on the cause.

For avoidance, it may be as simple as not liking to deal with others' emotional reactions. Explore what led to these circumstances and where you learned them. By allowing yourself an in-depth look at your patterns, you can break free of the bull that stands in your own way. Be brutally honest with yourself. Again, taking our example of avoidance, see what you can discover. Is it judgment? Not wanting to make a scene? Denying your own needs? Pretending that the problem will go away on its own? Wanting to feel righteous in being right? The possibilities are endless and personal.

- Create a game plan.

Once you've chopped, diced, and dissected why and in what instances your unconstructive patterns arise, create actions in order to break through them. It doesn't need to necessarily have to be about the pattern. Use your intuition to guide you toward the right solution. Ask your higher self what it needs. What you are trying to accomplish is giving yourself a moment before you go into your automated reaction. In creating this "third space," you empower yourself to take a moment to decide how you want to react. In learning from your patterns, you don't magically fix or outgrow them, but you do learn that you are not a slave to them, which leads to a more authentic, grounded, and supported you.

## WE'RE ALL A BUNCH OF NEEDY BEANS

Getting back in touch with yourself and what you need is the basis of not only your intuition but also your power. When you honor yourself by taking care of your needs, you move away from life happening "to you" and move into personal responsibility. When you know what your needs are, you don't look to others to fulfill them, and when you're clear about where you need to grow, you don't get dragged down in other people's energy. So the big question remains: What do you need, and how can you use your intuition to discover those needs?

When we start to slow down, become quiet, and turn off the noise of our lives, we may at first think, *It's just too quiet in here*, or *If I feel my emotions I might get overwhelmed*. It's so true. When we pause and start to look inward, it can feel intense and overwhelming. What might be lurking in the basement of our subconscious selves? What bogeymen might lie in wait?

Before you throw yourself on the floor in despair, remember that whether you're looking or not, these emotions and self-destructive patterns are there. Go easy on yourself and begin looking with a light(er) heart. You are by your very nature a creative, beautiful human being with a bright Spirit. The shitty patterns don't have to be the reason you feel bad in the world.

Ready? First, take some space. Sit down somewhere quiet and take a few breaths to get centered and quiet your mind. Next, turn your energy toward your heart and tune in to your intuition. Instead of making this seem impossible, just remember that your intuition is an unconscious connector—it's not going to be like the voice of God booming in your ear. Trust yourself and *listen*. Intuition in the simplest of terms is listening and receiving. Most important, trust the information you're receiving and don't let your ego fake you out. Remember, intuition isn't emotional but instead feels grounded. Now ask yourself, out loud, "What do I need?" Put a timer on for five minutes and just start talking. The reason to do it out loud is that the sound of your own voice is a powerful tool. Remember the inner ear, or cochlea, that we discussed in Chapter 1? The one that picks up on vibration? Think of it as your energetic bullshit meter. If it doesn't sound right, then it's not.

Continue questioning: "What makes me happy? Do I need people? Do I need space?" The biggest part of this exercise is to begin listening to yourself. Don't make it too complicated. Take a breath. Drop in. Look at times or places where you have been uncomfortable; look at your patterns objectively and lovingly. Don't blame, don't shame, don't let your ego take over. Your patterns can contain huge clues into finding out which needs aren't getting met. Where does life feel like it's lacking? At home? At work? In your personal relationships? When you detach from your ego, tune in to your intuition, and let your heart speak, you'll be surprised that you know exactly what you need, but only if you take the time and *listen*.

## HELP YOURSELF

- Consider where you are courageously tuned in . . . and where you're not.

- Explore your patterns. What is your go-to reaction or need? Do this lovingly.

- Look at *why* you do what you do. Without the *why*, you can't begin to fix the problem.

- Look for a common theme—maybe it's impatience, overgiving, sacrificing, escapism.

- Put your hand on your heart and speak it out loud. What do you need? What are you missing? When you say the words out loud, you'll start to train your heart to feel the vibration.

- Honor your own needs.

# CHAPTER 3

# YOU ARE AMAZING— NOW OWN IT

## LEARNING TO FALL WITH JAZZ HANDS

As we grow from children into adults, we tend to tune out our hearts and tune in to the chatter of the world. We might tune in to our egos, or the voice of our parents, society, a teacher, or our peers—and slowly we get in the habit of being critical of ourselves. We hear that little voice that says, *You can't do that,* and instead of saying, "Fuck that!" we believe our fear as fact. These self-limiting beliefs become the lens through which we view the world. Holding our self-judgment close, we start to compare ourselves to others or to our idealized image of ourselves. That pesky fear brain comes and whispers in our ears, *You know you're right,* or *Don't do that. You'll look so dumb and everyone will judge you.*

Your fearful brain wants to protect you. It doesn't want you to feel insecure and scared, so it tells you all these insane things to keep you in a small enough box to feel in control. But, in reality, there won't ever be enough security to satisfy the ego. It's like

an overprotective grandmother. She might have the best inten-
tions, but in trying to protect you, she traps you in the apartment
and tells you the world is a terrible place filled with scary diseases
and murderers. She forwards you horrifying news stories when
you're relaxing with your friends about how people die in unusual
ways, especially when they're relaxing with their friends.

We have grown up in a society where we're not allowed to
make mistakes. We have been cultivated and rewarded for the
"right" answer, whether it be in school, at work, or with friends.
This system of right and wrong sets up a problem—we're human
beings and we're going to make mistakes. But, unfortunately,
when we make those mistakes, we don't look at them as learning experiences but rather as failures—and it's bad. This creates
shame, one of the most powerful and damaging emotions, and
makes us feel disconnected from one another.

Can we let you in on a little secret? Everyone is insecure.
We are human beings having a messy human experience. We all
want to fit in and be loved. But if we start to think these self-
defeating beliefs are true, they become true. From our experience and being on the ground level with so many of our clients,
we see this as an epidemic. It kills our creativity, our passion,
and because like attracts like, we end up surrounded by people
who cannot believe that we can do more. Because our experience informs our reality, we find ourselves in a loop of belief that
whatever we are reaching for is impossible or foolish. We find
ourselves giving away our power to the peanut gallery, subconsciously living our lives for "them."

While your ego chatters away, your mind quivers in the corner, afraid because it won't ever have enough information to feel
truly safe. The mind is like a black hole in space because by its
very design, it wants to *understand*. The issue here is that to have
a truly intuitive life, we won't be able to fully understand our intuition. There have been countless times in our lives that we have
made really important decisions based purely on the voice of our
gut. Though our minds were confused and anxious, we knew that

our intuition could be trusted, even if what it was telling us to do didn't "make sense."

The mind can be your worst enemy because by wanting to figure everything out, it removes the magical unknown elements of living an intuitive life. Our minds like to think things through because we've been told that's the responsible approach. In school, we aren't urged to daydream. We're asked to focus. We're encouraged not only to think inside the box but also to think inside the box someone else built. It's not even our box!

Making choices out of fear rarely, if ever, has amazing results. We know that if we let our minds be the sole decision makers, we would be two stuck and frustrated young women. After all, it's the mind's job to draw conclusions and judge. Your mind judges the world around you, but it especially judges *you*. Now, really, how hard is it to make a choice or take a risk when you feel judged? Are you doing some serious judging of yourself right now?

Truly magical and miraculous things come when you listen to the voice of your gut and take action. Recently, we were watching television and a doctor was performing brain surgery on a man. What was amazing was that the man being operated on was fully awake. Eyes open. Blinking. Talking. He was awake because his brain couldn't *feel* the operation. The brain doesn't have nerve-feeling receptors the way your heart or your stomach do. Thus, your brain just is not the place you need to go when you need to tune in to your intuition. It literally doesn't connect. Your feelings come from your heart and your gut. The mind then interprets the information, and from this place, you make a decision.

The mind doesn't want to believe in magic because then it has to give up control. It has to surrender to a power greater than itself. Give yourself permission to fail miserably—spectacularly!—and do it with pride. It takes courage to allow yourself to be messy and give up the illusion of control. It will feel amazing, like if you had been clenching your butt cheeks for years and you finally unclenched. If your inner grandma starts to ramble on, give her a squeeze and tell her, *It's okay, we're just learning.*

## BE BIG, BABY

Playing small is a common result of listening to our self-limiting, ego-driven beliefs. It means downplaying accomplishments, goals, achievements, or beliefs in order to make others feel more comfortable. It is a form of caretaking that does nothing to serve us or those around us. How do we play small? We do it all the time—as a way to make conversation or to make sure we don't come off as cocky. We have been told that we shouldn't "brag," but in reality, celebrating our successes and bragging are two very different things.

When we play small, we will never be pretty enough, smart enough, or happy enough, and we look outside of ourselves for validation. We deny ourselves and our successes and give others the power to tell us if we're "okay" or not. This is a plague in our society. In our competitive world, we're always told to look to others to know if we're "succeeding." We have many friends who play small in their lives in all sorts of ways, whether it means staying in a job that they hate or not challenging themselves to try new things. We're all human and we all have our own insecurities, but when we play small, we let those insecurities run the show, limiting ourselves.

Sometimes, we become angry and subconsciously undercut others who are making different choices, or we get mad at ourselves, thinking that we could never do something like that. Playing small takes on many forms—in its essence, it's giving away our power to others.

---

## WE'RE HAVING FUN, RIGHT?

*At a friend's party, I met a lovely woman who had the sweetest energy. However, I found that throughout our* entire conversation, she kept making small quips about herself. I complimented her on her top and she countered by saying that it did not fit right. We talked about her work as a musical consultant and she said she was just the head of the company and the real genius was her team of employees. She made jokes at her own expense, over and over again. After a while, it became uncomfortable.

The whole conversation revolved around how defunct she was and how amazing everyone else was. She'd learned to play small as a way to relate to others. She couldn't allow herself any sort of success in case it detracted from someone else. From an energetic perspective, you could tell that she was suffering and that these comments were real truths that she believed and were then reinforced through the laughter that they evoked. But, even on the other side, it was superboring. I didn't want to spend the entire conversation reassuring her or acknowledging these false and misguided attempts to connect. Instead of sharing her gifts, passion for music, and sweet energy, she created a wall between herself and others. Her own insecurities ran so deep that she had gotten herself stuck in a pattern of playing small.

After talking to her for 45 minutes, I finally called her out on it. I asked her point-blank: "Why do you keep putting yourself down?" Shocked at the question, she was taken aback for a moment. She stammered: "I don't like cocky people because I find them to be obnoxious. No one wants to hear you brag about yourself. I'm just trying to be humble."

I don't think she liked my question. What she failed to realize was that she was being obnoxious because not only was she playing small, but she was forcing everyone else to find ways to cater to her insecurities. In searching for affirmation that she was as terrible as she made herself out to be *or reinforcement that she was just as good as everyone else, she was putting herself down over and over again for others to walk all over her. She didn't even realize it, but she had bad vibes and became a doormat for everyone around her.*

---

We're not used to a culture that celebrates one another. Instead, we're used to constantly comparing ourselves to magazines, to Instagram, to whatever it is. When we play small, we hide what we want, who we are, the gifts we bring, and our unique badassery. The thing about people who don't play small is that they shine and remind us that we can too. People who have that magic know who they are and don't need anyone else to define them. (Hello, Beyoncé!) They know who they are. When we share our gifts, our creations, and our joy, connected to our hearts, and live without apology, we reconnect to our power.

So how do you stop playing small? To begin, what do you say to yourself? Do you allow yourself to make mistakes? Or do you berate yourself? Do you forgive yourself and move on? The majority of people are incredibly hard on themselves.

Step one: don't be an asshole to yourself. Pay attention to how you talk to yourself. Life is hard; you don't need to make it harder. Instead of being hard on yourself, start to counter those feelings with compassion. Be kind to yourself when you make mistakes, when you feel scared, when you don't know what to do. When that chatter starts up again, pay attention to the vibration. Being mindful is a huge step. So often we are on autopilot, that when we are mindful about what we are thinking, we disrupt the pattern. When we take a moment and recognize, *Jeez, that's really harsh*, we start to create room for a new way to do it. Ask yourself: *If my best friend called me, would I say to them what I am saying to myself?*

Your voice is a powerful tool. When you catch yourself playing small, vocalize what you're thinking. Feel the vibration. Take a
moment and then ask yourself, *Is that true?*

If you can, actually talk about what you're thinking with your
most supportive friend—someone who reminds you that you're
wonderful just the way you are. It can be scary to open up and
talk about our insecurities, but when we allow ourselves to be
real about life, it connects us. Whenever we're on the struggle
bus, we call each other and just let it all hang out. And we feel better, even if the "problem" isn't fixed. It becomes smaller and way
more manageable. When we face our problem and fears, they no
longer subconsciously motivate us. Fear is not a great motivator;
it taps into our limbic nervous system, the reptilian part of our
brain that controls fight, flight, freeze, and floods our system with
cortisol—the stress hormone.

Our mom always said, "It isn't fear that's stopping you; it's
hiding fear." There is a lot of power in being real and talking about
what makes us feel scared or crazy or where we are insecure.
When we hide our mistakes, what we believe to be our inad-
equacies, we slowly sap our energy and numb ourselves from
the world. Hiding them or pretending that they aren't there isn't
going to make them go away. It's like having an open wound and
thinking if you ignore it, it will go away. (It won't.)

Start to connect to who you *are*. Not your personality but
those things you know to be true about yourself, no matter what.
You were born with so many gifts. You have a unique amazing-
ness that you're here to share with the world. If you have trouble
thinking about the things that make you magical, start by looking
at your best friend. What are all those things that you just love
about him or her? Now start to think about yourself. What are the
things that you know you're good at? What are the things you do
that make you put down your phone and lose track of time? Once
you start to pull that thread, you'll begin to remind yourself of
how amazing you are. It's not boastful or prideful; it's important.

It's like watering your own garden. Playing "big" doesn't mean walking around like Kanye, saying, "I'm the shit and you'll never be as awesome as me." It's saying, "I'm the shit because I'm awesome—and so are you."

In our culture we are taught to believe that we cannot be successful without the proper training. In order to work in business, we need to go to business school. To be an artist, you need to go to art school. Doodlers need not apply. We obsess about training, internships, and in the process create all the roadblocks imaginable to our dreams. We have forgotten to just get in there and do it. Don't play small. Don't pretend that you can't, or make up a million reasons why it won't work out. We're really good at not even trying because we've already imagined a million and one ways that it won't work. The only things that stand between you and your dreams are creativity, hard work, and the belief that you can do whatever you want, no matter what. It might not be exactly what you imagined, but it'll be even better. You are good enough, smart enough, and creative enough—and don't let yourself or anybody else tell you otherwise!

## CALM YOUR CRAZY

Turn on the news: terrorism, the environment, mass shootings, high unemployment rates, debt, global warming—the list of menacing things is never-ending. The constant message is "be scared." Fear is the loudest voice in our culture right now, and it affects our consciousness. We pick up on these messages—whether it be that you're not safe or you're not going to get a job or you're always going to be in debt. It can even just be an undercurrent of fearful energy that makes you feel like you're not doing a good enough job in life. We've become infected with fear.

Full disclosure: we're sensitive, anxious people too. It's not like we've got it all locked down and now we're just floating through life. You should spend an hour with the two of us. We talk about our anxieties and fears without hesitation because they're real and they're powerful. But we just don't make our choices from that place. We acknowledge the fears and then connect to our hearts.

An easy exercise you can do to actually hear the difference between your fears and your heart is to talk out loud in the voice of each. (Your voice sounds so good.) So many times we spend hours thinking, hoping that we'll come to some sort of satisfactory conclusion after we've thought it over enough. This process is both draining and time-consuming.

So instead, do what we do when we're feeling superstuck. Next time you're freaking out about something, or you're really in need of some guidance from your intuition, put one hand on your heart and one hand on your belly. Start by breathing all the way into your belly and exhaling out the sound "Ahhhhh."

Do this a few times to unlock your voice. Actually force the sound out if it's stuck. Laughter sometimes comes just from this part. Let it. Now wiggle your hips a bit, back and forth. Just be in your body. Next, out loud, fill in the next prompts.

"My head says_____."
"And my heart says _____."

Go back and forth, actually listening out loud to both your head and your heart speak. The voice of your heart isn't going to be as talkative as your head. Sometimes, we do this and we get one or two words from our heart. But the grounded, courageous voice of our hearts is enough to calm our minds down and help us make a sound decision. If you really give it your all, what comes out of your mouth when you give your heart the floor might really surprise you.

### Sabrina Temporarily Loses Her Mind

Recently, I called my sister at two in the morning having an anxiety-induced freak-out. I had convinced myself that the guy I was interested in was ignoring me on Facebook. I spent my night obsessing over what he had said, how I had responded, and how I hadn't heard back from him. A perfectly innocent conversation had sent me spiraling down into a hole of despair. I told myself that his silence was actually disinterest. While the night deepened, along with my lunacy, I wrote an insane message declaring that I was, in fact, no longer interested in him. I told myself I KNEW how he felt and that I would need to take action by giving him a good old-fashioned piece of my mind. Fear had taken over, and I decided I had to do something to get myself out of feeling so upset.

Now, before I sent him my message, my Spirit told me to call my sister. I hesitated. It was late. She answered the phone on the first ring. "I knew something was up. I just woke up from a crazy dream where you were running in a circle." (She's a Pisces; these prophetic dreams happen often.) "What's wrong?"

I was shaking. "My gut tells me that he's not interested!" I shrieked into the phone, louder than was appropriate and definitely insensitive to the fact that she was patient enough to answer my call in the first place.

"Take a deep breath. Listen to me. That is not your intuition speaking. That's your fear. I know it's easy to get the two confused, especially at two in the morning when you're all worked up and trolling Facebook. Trust me. Go to bed.

Turn off Facebook. We can decide in the morning how to approach this. Breathe."

I took a deep breath in through the nose and exhaled through my mouth, just like blowing out a birthday candle. I protested for a few more moments, but hearing the sound of my own voice trying to justify my craziness made it clear: I had jumped on the midnight express to Crazy Town and needed to get off before I made things worse for myself.

Sonia was right. What I had done was confuse my emotions with my intuition.

You might be thinking to yourself: Sabrina, you're a professional counselor and psychic! Shouldn't you know the difference between your inner crazy and your intuition? Here is the truth: being conscious and intuitive doesn't mean that I get to bypass the growing pains of insecurity. I might be able to tell the difference for a friend or a client, but when I'm in the middle of a midnight meltdown, my intuition isn't going to prevent me from my anxious, crazy feelings.

Here is the golden rule: breathe. When emotions run high, it's common for emotion and intuition to feel fused together. What I know works is when I press pause, take a deep breath, calm down, and drink a glass of water.

So, after having the gift of a sister grounded enough to slap me around and calm me down, I hung up the phone, put away my laptop, and started breathing in through my nose and out through my mouth. This breath calms the nervous system and relaxes the mind. It calmed the part of my brain that told me I wasn't safe, or that I needed to be aware of danger and take action.

*I slowly drifted to sleep and woke up the next morning to (surprise!) a Facebook message from the guy! He had lost his Internet connection, and that was his reason for going missing.*

*Despite being intuitive, and even for the most part confident, I still need to keep my mind and my crazy in check.*

---

## I'M SO GREAT PARTY

What we tell ourselves is true about the world is true about the world. The message here is that our own beliefs are powerful enough to create an experience that informs how the universe treats and reacts to us.

Limiting self-beliefs will tear you down faster than any outside force. Our friend Patrick traveled the world as a writer for a successful magazine he started. Every time we connected, he would be in a fabulous five-star hotel somewhere different. Despite this seemingly fabulous life, he was absolutely unfulfilled. He spent his time living someone else's dream job because he was too afraid to pursue his own. His dream was to be a comedy writer, and he had written a short film that he'd never shared with anyone. When asked why he hid his talent for comedy from the world, Patrick responded that no one had ever told him he was funny.

This struck us as such a powerful statement in its simplicity. The truth is, in order to achieve success and joy, we have to be open to our own gifts and talents first. When we wait for other people to validate us, we're putting our worth and joy in their hands, and who knows how clear they are to even see our gifts in the first place?

Patrick needed to throw himself what we like to call an I'm So Great Party. The only rules of this party are that you are absolutely willing to talk about how great you are. Without reservation, list why you are just truly and unabashedly great. It goes something like this: "I'm such a great artist. I am such a great student. I am a great daughter. I am a great lover of life. I am great at seeing other people's gifts. I am great at communicating. I am great at uplifting others. I am really great at matching a fabulous pair of shoes with my outfit."

You are the one who knows your gifts and your talents. You know where you are unique and where you contribute. You know where you are absolutely fantastically awesome and unbelievably beautiful.

At first Patrick struggled with our party plan. In his mind, it sounded less like an I'm So Great Party and more like a bragging hoedown. However, with a few more encouraging "Who cares? We're the only ones here," and "We can do this AA style" statements, he began slowly listing where he felt he was truly great. To his surprise, once the words began to come, he was like a moving train, gaining momentum and confidence with each "I'm so great!"

One of the greatest sicknesses in the world is that people have been conditioned to self-analyze and criticize without any hesitation at all. We say some of the worst and downright painful things to ourselves. This creates a pattern of self-criticism between our own ears that can be staggeringly hateful. In order to achieve a truly whole and happy life, we have to start by recognizing our honest gifts and talents, unabashedly screaming from the rooftops why we're incredible. Forget where you feel ugly. Forget when you feel stupid. Forget that time you made an ass of yourself.

Instead, make a commitment to change the dialogue between your ears. The fastest road out of self-hating, mean-spirited Crazy Town is a strong dose of "I'm so great!"

## HELP YOURSELF

- Don't put yourself down for conversational value. It's boring and it's not true!

- Don't be a dick to yourself. Instead, share your awesomeness and see people for their gifts as well.

- Celebrate how wonderful you are with daily affirmations. Use a dry-erase marker and write things on your bathroom mirror.

- Put a baby picture of yourself as your screen saver and ask yourself, *Would I tell that to me if I were a baby?*

- Be honest about what scares you. Answer the following out loud: "If I weren't afraid, I would

  _____."

- If you're really struggling with your self-esteem and can't seem to feel like you're okay, talk to a therapist who can help you untangle some of these deep-seated beliefs.

- Take care of your Spirit! Remember, when we feed ourselves, even for just a few minutes a day, we start to become more sensitive to what our Spirit needs.

- Get a good support system—friends and family who know and support how awesome you are. It doesn't have to be a party: one good, honest friend can help you shine your gifts on the world.

- Use your voice; it's a powerful tool. Say what you're thinking OUT LOUD. Put your hand on your heart and ask yourself: *Is this true? Does it resonate?* Chances are, it doesn't.

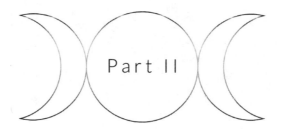

Part II

# SPIRIT, YOUR NEW BESTIE

# CHAPTER 4

# BREAKING OUT OF YOUR COMFORT ZONE

Growing up is hard. Being an adult is hard. Being a conscious adult is even harder. Don't you remember being a kid and thinking that when you were an adult, you'd have everything figured out? We do. There was this romantic idea that once you crossed into adulthood, life would just become magically easy. Wouldn't it be nice if that were real life? As we all know by now, things only get *more* complicated. Let's not pretend it's all "good"—life can be shitty sometimes. Whether it's breaking up with your significant other, changing your major or job, moving to another city, or even just getting older, sometimes life feels like it's never going to get better. When things generally feel like a never-ending suck fest, it can be tempting to feel like a victim, and like life is happening to you and there is nothing you can do about it. On one level, that's true. There is much we can't control—but when shit gets real, we do have a choice. We can connect with our hearts, our Spirits, our higher selves—or disconnect.

Don't get us wrong. We can still feel how we're feeling—whether it's anger, sadness, fear—but we can't let those feelings be the captain of our ship. They are terrible drivers. Sometimes what happens is we freeze, not wanting to make yet another wrong move. Disconnected from our hearts, our fragile egos can go into overdrive—*Don't do that; it's not safe!* When we're already in vulnerable territory and cut off from our Spirit, the ego is an easy voice to listen to. Couple that with all the other voices that are all too happy to remind us that the world is unfair and we're not safe, and we've got lots of perfectly good reasons to never leave our rooms again. If we choose to listen only to those voices, the world becomes smaller and smaller.

We're a different, superconnected generation with smartphones, a constant connection to the Internet amplifying to us an uncertain economy, a tough job market, terrorism, student debt, institutional racism, and we're broadcasting it on the Internet, all the time—the list goes on and on. The message is the same: you're screwed, so stay where it's safe. But on a deeper level, we want more. That feeling is your Spirit tugging at you, saying, *Let's go play, let's explore, let's do something different, you're safe, we got this.* When you connect to your Spirit, nurture your relationship with your heart and yourself, you tune out the noise of the world and tune in to infinite wisdom. Nine times out of ten, people know exactly what they want—they just need to quiet the voices of their egos or the world enough to listen.

We get scared to listen to our intuition because we think if we tune in to it, we're obligated to follow it. But you're a grown-up, so, frankly, you can do whatever you want. Like with all things, you have a choice. The worst thing that will happen? Nothing—your life will stay the same.

We're not going to lie: choosing to trust your intuition requires a serious amount of courage. Of course we want to protect ourselves from upset, pain, or disappointment. No one in his or her right mind wants to charge into chaos. We're usually trying to find strategies to protect us from uncomfortable feelings. But when we constantly try to avoid discomfort, and close ourselves off from all the "scary" or "bad" things in the world, we end up closing ourselves off from all the good stuff too. Choosing to tune inward and connect to our hearts opens up a whole other dimension where we're in charge. We discover that we're endlessly powerful and creative and fucking awesome. Tough things become things we can learn from. We can grow and make choices that serve us.

We start to reframe things and learn from them. We learn that we're not powerless but rather endlessly powerful. For example, let's say your SO does, in fact, dump you. You're heartbroken and just wanting relief. When you're connected to your ego, it can go one of two ways: you tell yourself, *There is something fundamentally wrong with me! I don't deserve love and it's all my fault!* Or you may do a 180 and think, *Screw that guy. He's the worst and it's all his fault. I'm never going to date again!*

After a heartbreak, of course we can have these feelings. Our egos do everything they can to protect us from pain. We want to feel like we're in control, like we know the answer. But how do those things feel? We feel contracted, closed off, and nothing moves. The reason why the energy doesn't move is that the left (logic) and right (emotional) hemispheres do not connect. So we can use our left brain and come up with all the logic in the world, but it won't make us feel better.

Let's take that same breakup and look at it from the point of view of our Spirit. The heartbreak and pain are still there. It still sucks. But the conversation takes on a different tone: we *feel* our feelings without intellectualizing them. *My heart hurts. I'm sad. I'm mad.* As we move through our grief, we can start to process what happened. We can connect the left and right hemispheres of our brain. We look at what we learned from the relationship. What were the good things? What were the not-so-good things? New thoughts can drop in, like, *That guy was totally emotionally unavailable. In my next relationship, I want someone who doesn't make my emotions wrong.* Or even, in simple terms, *He was just not right for me. I don't totally get it right now, but I know that there is something I need to learn here. It's all going to work out, even if I don't feel like that right now.*

When connecting to your Spirit, you're able to see yourself and your life from a different perspective. You can see that you're a soul on a journey. You're not a victim. You empower yourself to change the story and keep yourself open to new things. Let's be clear: it's not a silver bullet or a spiritual bypass. We can't just spiritualize all the shit that happens and make our problems disappear. That's the intellect faking us out. When you're connected to your Spirit, you feel the fear, but you don't let it call the shots. You allow it to move through you because you're safe and anchored in your Spirit. You know you're connected and that *you* get to decide.

## GIVING YOURSELF THE GO-AHEAD

We laugh when people ask us if growing up in our home was calm and peaceful because our parents knew how to meditate. If anything, our family is loud and intense, and we wear our emotions and feelings on the outside. It was like growing up in a nudist colony. Everyone was connected, and nothing was off-limits to talk about. This especially applied to the feeling of fear.

Instead of hiding our fears, we were encouraged to address them head on. We know how unique it is that we were able to talk about our anxieties and what was the freak-out du jour. We could feel, and talk about, what we were afraid of until the feeling passed and we felt better. We called it "emptying the garbage."

If you want a badass life, you need to feel your fears and then do whatever it is you are afraid of *anyway.* Life, and especially the unknown, can feel scary. But if we change our perspective, our fear can be turned into adventure. Newness and adventure can feel overwhelming or terrifying when you've been pushed outside of your normal comfort zone. Have you ever moved to a new city? Or started a new job? Or taken that zip-lining course even though you're terrified of heights? We all have those *Oh, shit, what am I doing?* moments. But once we do them, we can look back and say, *That wasn't so bad.* Fear will keep you in a corner, waiting for permission to live your life.

The catch? The only person who can ever assure you to feel your fears and live life anyway is you. No one else can connect to your heart or give you permission to live full out. Don't ignore your fears—it won't work. Instead, get grounded in your Spirit, feel that fear, and do it anyway. (Unless you're literally in danger, then GTFO.)

When we were in Costa Rica on a family trip, our driver strongly suggested that we hire a boat to take us out onto the ocean to see the natural park in all its glory. Now, we aren't exactly what you'd call "boat people." Afraid, but intrigued by the adventure, the three of us climbed aboard a small boat and set out into the bay on a particularly windy day in December. The sun was glistening over the ocean, and with each bounce of the boat, we were all a little green. Our live-it-out-loud, face-your-fears, fabulous mother was literally gripping the side of the boat for dear life.

About 20 minutes into the trip, our captain, a tall and gregarious Costa Rican man, began to pick up speed. Suddenly, we saw what the captain was rushing toward. Out in the bay was a baby whale jumping enthusiastically, leaping into the water, turning over, back up and over again. This little baby whale was playing full out. She was having a great time, and every so often we would see the baby whale's mother slowly surface to reveal her truly enormous back. Facing our fear was rewarded with a profoundly magical gift from the universe. Even our captain couldn't believe our luck. It was extremely rare to see them so close.

Okay, so you may recognize that your fear is holding you back. Now what? *I'm freaking terrified to jump into my dreams, ladies, because it might not work out for me.* Well, we're all in the same boat. But isn't any life worth living a tiny bit scary? Just a little?

---

### SONIA'S HO CHI MINH ADVENTURE

*When we graduated from college, a couple of my classmates were planning a trip to Southeast Asia for three months. Andrew and Kenneth were best friends. We ran in the same social circles, we hung out, we were friends but we weren't supertight. During a house party they were throwing, I started asking them about their trip. It sounded awesome! I'd always wanted to go backpacking, so when Andrew looked at me and said: "Wanna come?" I had a decision to make. With a little liquid courage in my system—a potent combination of excitement, nervousness, and adrenaline fueled by a few drinks—I felt ready to say yes but wanted to make sure it was a sincere invite.*

*"Are you sure? Because I totally would!" I said.*

*"We wouldn't invite you if we weren't."*

*All right, I was going. I was pumped to be heading to Asia for three months, but I was also terrified. First off, they were best friends and boys—was I going to be the odd one out? I'd always spent time with ladies. How would I adjust to being with only boys 24/7? What if I got there and they realized they had made a big mistake? What if I was too needy? What if I got supersick and we had to share a bathroom? What if I didn't like the food? What if we fought? The list of stuff that could go wrong grew. I had to spend all the money I had made* babysitting for a special-needs child to go on a trip with two boys who I didn't know that well. For three months. But the trip felt right—even if my ego wondered if I had lost my damn mind. I talked to my parents, and they agreed to help me with the flight as a graduation gift. My ticket purchased, the guys and I agreed we would all meet in Ho Chi Minh City.

Fast-forward to the end of summer. The plane landed in Vietnam at 1 A.M. Walking out of the airport, I was surrounded by total chaos. Exhausted and jet-lagged, I was a tad freaked out, to put it mildly. Had I really just flown to the other side of the world to meet up with two dudes I hardly knew? Had we really agreed that we would coordinate meeting up via e-mail? My brain would not shut up. Vietnam is very different from the U.S.—at 1 A.M. the streets were packed with people, which was such a departure from Portland. I saw three people riding the same moped, carrying two huge suitcases. Culture shock set in as I rode on the back of a motorbike with my giant backpack, weaving through traffic. I just wanted to get to my hostel, sleep, and find them in the morning.

All of a sudden, being alone made me want to turn around and go back to the airport. What had I done? How did my parents let me do this? Once we pulled up to the hostel, everything went awry. They had lost my reservation, there was a conference in town, and everything was booked. There was nothing they or any other hostel within 20 miles could do. And to top it all off, it was now 3 A.M. and I had just traveled for more than 24 hours. Panicked, I called my dad, sobbing. He calmed me down, told me to go to a hotel—he would foot the bill—get some sleep, and regroup in the morning.

I awoke in a hotel room and e-mailed Andrew and Kenneth. After a few hours, I still didn't hear back from them.

*The fear crept in, and my intellect started to fill in the blanks. They hadn't actually want me to come. They were going to ditch me. I had just made a HUGE mistake. Self-conscious, scared, and alone, I kept refreshing my e-mail.*

*Hours later, I received word that they had traveled down to another city an hour away and I could meet them if I wanted. I froze. I was stranded in Vietnam, and that's when the fear got louder and louder until it was deafening. Half of me thought,* Fuck this, I'm going to travel alone and I'm going to love it. *The other part of me said,* Run away, go home! *I called my parents, who told me if I wanted to come home I could. I was going to think it over. I headed out on a cry walk through the city, returned back to my room, booked another night, and told my family I was going to come home. All of those things I was scared of had come true, my scared brain told me. I was right, it reminded me.*

*But there was a teeny-tiny part of me that wasn't believing my scared self. The voice of my mom came into my brain:* What does your Spirit say? *Like a true daughter, the fear part of me didn't want to listen to my mom.* She doesn't know anything, *my brain told me.*

*I decided to check in with my Spirit. I was so tuned in to my fear I could hardly hear it. At first, all I felt was my anxiety, which tensed my shoulders, made my throat feel constricted, and made my heart pound. I knew I needed to get grounded. What was I really afraid of? So I took a breath and then another and another. I put my hand on my heart and started emptying the "trash," out loud.*

*As I voiced what was so loud in my brain, I could feel what was fear and what was real. Would these guys really invite me halfway around the world, only to ditch me? Nope,*

*that was the fear talking. As I heard my thoughts out loud,*
*I could tell I was listening to a scared, crazy person. After*
*a while I finally asked myself,* What am I really afraid of?
*The grounded voice of my intuition answered,* You're just
uncomfortable and feeling out of control. Go. *With that, I*
*knew I needed to go. I needed to feel my fear, my discomfort,*
*and go anyway. So, I took a deep breath and did. I managed*
*to find a local bus to the hostel they were staying at in a town*
*that did not cater to tourists, and I found my friends. It was*
*incredible. Kenneth and Andrew are now two of my best*
*friends. I learned I'm a badass and I can be scared, but my*
*fear doesn't have to be in control. I'm so glad I didn't go home.*

---

We're going to feel fear. But when we connect to our Spirit, we can start to differentiate between what is scary because it's a leap of faith, different, or uncomfortable, and what is simply not for us. The reason why it's so important to build your connection to your heart and your Spirit through your own daily practice is that when scary situations come up, you can tell if it's just fear that stopping you or if it just isn't for you.

Over time, we can get really comfortable in the familiar, and stuck in old patterns. That's how ruts happen: doing the same thing unconsciously over and over, but desiring something different. It's also the definition of *crazy*. Changing the familiar is scary, but when we feel the tug, underneath it is likely the truth that we're not satisfied. A strong connection to our Spirit allows us to trust ourselves and our decisions.

Life is a constant stream of decisions, and you are a powerful being by definition. You create your own experience whether you are consciously doing so or not. Each moment is a creation, so our challenge to you is to create something great. That said, when you start to see yourself as a magician, a creator in the world who has influence, it can feel overwhelming.

Recently, we were working with our client Miranda, who was 49 years old and wanting to create a romantic relationship and find her passion. As a child, she had lost her father, and the effect it had on her was profound. Fear kept her stuck in a pattern that no longer served any purpose, and she felt powerless against the world.

In order to get unstuck, she first needed to realize that she was powerful. She had spent her life feeling like something was missing and that she was to blame. She held herself to an impossibly high standard and bullied herself into submission. Her fears told her that she wasn't ever going to find a partner and that her life was being wasted. Yet, despite this constant barrage of negative self-talk, Miranda had an urge to find herself again. She was sick of listening to the voice that told her to stay put. She wanted to explore the world and longed to travel.

When asked what her Spirit wanted, she immediately blurted out, "Adventure!" The answer surprised us all, and we started to laugh. But just as her Spirit was starting to wake up and voice itself, her brain butted in and immediately began a laundry list of every reason why she couldn't go: "I have work. I have bills to pay. I have to be responsible. I have no one to go with."

We could see her intellect grasping at straws, trying to come up with a reason to stay stuck where she was. Yet her Spirit wanted adventure.

"Miranda, whatever scares you most, go there first! Life is too short to try and stay comfortable and safe. You know what the worst thing that will happen to you is?" Sabrina asked.

"I'll lose everything and make a mistake?" she replied, hoping we would validate her fears.

"No, the worst possible thing that could happen to you is that nothing at all will happen and that you'll spend the rest of your life stuck exactly where you are now." This was the truth. Living life may be scary, but living stuck in a rut and unhappy is truly ter-rifying. Boredom is the slow leak in a boat that can take a person down if they're not paying attention. It doesn't happen all at once, but there comes a point where there is no light left in the eyes and no smile on the face. This is when fear of change wins over courage and adventure. And that's the worst fate of all!

When we listen to our inner voice, the Spirit moves us to make choices that lead to a fun and happy life. Without joy, life is dull. Spirit is spice and color, adventure and travel. To be inspired, by definition, means to bring the Spirit into something, and living an inspired life is fun.

So where does this leave us? Well, look at where you let your fear stop you. Where do you listen to the no of your own intellect instead of pushing yourself outside your comfort zone, into a new experience?

---

## Emergency! Emergency!

*My dad used to get us motivated by exclaiming, "Bail out! Bail out! This is not a drill." This happened mostly when arriving at a destination or when we were running late for school. To my father, this was a cute way to get Sonia and me moving. To me, however, it felt like we were constantly in a state of emergency.*

*As a child, I rarely slept and couldn't relax. I spent most nights lying awake in my room, staring up at the ceiling, wait-ing for the moment my mom's nightstand light went off so I knew she was tired enough not to fight my getting into bed with her.*

*Needless to say, this caused issues in our house. My mom was exhausted, and I was terrified. I was scared of* pretty much anything and everything that I had to do alone. I strategized about ways to avoid being by myself and even mastered the art of the self-induced bellyaches. Stress was a great way to get my body all out of sorts of things and make sure I was well taken care of.

So, my mom, exhausted and determined to help me become more self-confident, set out to develop what we called my "grounding system." Mostly, this meant I would be reminded to "get grounded" on a regular basis. In order to get grounded, we first had to understand what ungrounded me. Not eating the right foods, not getting enough sleep, or not following through on my responsibilities was the beginning. Exercise was fundamental, especially walking. Getting my body feeling good was step one. I needed to make sure I was getting the ABCs of what I needed.

The result of the "get grounded" campaign was a routine that I use to get myself relaxed and centered to this day. Here is my system. It starts with deep circular breathing, an Epsom salt bath, a clean pair of comfortable pajamas, and a good, funny book. If I am still not able to get myself grounded, I always remember to breathe. Knowing what gets you grounded in life is absolutely fundamental to being able to hear your intuition or make good, self-loving choices.

I know that not everyone is blessed with the joys of an overactive nervous system, but even so I find that most people are fried and have very few tools to get centered. It's only after they are facedown on the floor, a small white flag in their hands, that they are willing to admit a need to get centered. Self-care isn't a luxury. I know for myself that it is the ground level, the very foundation, to living a good life.

Life is a constant stream of choices. *Do I jump into this or out? Do I play the edges or decide to feel scared, fearful, or uncomfortable and do it anyway?* Our society is literally obsessed with comfort—and it's overrated. Go to any mall in America and you can spend thousands of dollars being more comfortable that you currently are. Even jeans are made of leggings now. Comfort has a time and a place, but if it gets out of control our lives become one large, suffocating down pillow. We can't be so obsessed with comfort at the expense of adventure.

You know the term *growing pains*? Well, growing up is uncomfortable. What this book asks you to do might make you uncomfortable because it's different. We're creatures of habit. And furthermore, our generation is the first to have grown up with smartphones, instant messaging, Yelp, memory foam mattresses . . . you catch my drift. The issue with being obsessed with comfort is that we've seen our peers stop growing as soon as it feels hard because they're afraid that the discomfort is a bad sign. It's not a bad sign. Get good at being uncomfortable. It'll serve you in the long run. You'll have a much bigger and richer life from this one awareness.

## HELP YOURSELF

- Check in with yourself. Ask yourself if you're afraid or if you shouldn't do something because it's not supportive to your Spirit.

- Get a grounding routine that works for you.

- Pay attention to your body. How does it feel? Are your shoulders tense? Is your breathing deep or shallow? When we carry stress and fear, it physically manifests in our bodies. Create a check-in system and do it throughout the day.

- Be okay with being uncomfortable. It means you're learning.

- Set goals. Always wanted to travel? Try a dance class? Learn a new skill? Then go do it and be okay with being a little scared. New things aren't easy!

- Write down your successes. It's easy for our intellects to dismiss our successes, and when we can look back and see what we've accomplished it gives us courage to step into the unknown.

- Don't forget to breathe. When we get scared, the first thing we do is hold our breath. Put your hand on your belly, breathe deeply, and ground yourself into the room.

CHAPTER 5

# BAD VIBES

## WHAT SMELLS IN HERE?

Living on planet Earth means sometimes dealing with the crappy parts of life. We all have our off days, or even weeks for that matter, where we're in the dumps and need our friends and family to help build us up. An important part of deep relationships is the ability to let ourselves be vulnerable and perhaps even negative, if that's the way we're authentically feeling. Being real about where we are allows energy to move through us and not get stuck like a stagnant pond. But we don't want to get high on bad vibes, constantly throwing shade like a bunch of haters or complaining incessantly. The challenge is to find where these natural ups and downs of life turn into a negative bad-vibe cycle.

We are composed of a complex system of parts. Some of these parts are amazing and beautiful, and we want the whole world to see them. They're bright and shiny and cute. These are our gifts. The other part of being human is what we call our "shadow." It's the shit we hide under our beds and hope to God no one notices. Our shadows can be our jealous tendencies, our critical minds, our self-hatred and self-sabotage. A shadow is like a silent-but-deadly fart: it kind of creeps up on you from time to time, and you hope that no one around you notices.

When we feel bad vibes, their source is usually someone who got stuck in the negative energy cycles of their own shadow. Because of this funky shadow energy they feel on the inside, they start to project that funk out into the world. As receptive human beings, we pick up on the energy they're putting down, and we can become the victims of bad-vibe attacks and energy vampires. It's like getting caught in someone's energetic indigestion. As the incredible, wonderful, amazing human you are, you've got some basic rights—such as not having to get energetically slimed or taken advantage of, and maintaining healthy boundaries. So let's get down to brass tacks and talk about bad vibes and boundaries.

## TAKE COVER

Is this a familiar situation? You had a wonderful morning, maybe you even ate your favorite breakfast and went for a run, but then by lunch you feel as though you're going to punch your co-worker in the mouth if they utter a syllable to you. Have you ever been in a situation and just felt like *I need to get out of here right now* for no apparent reason? It's as though a fog has moved in; you went from having a perfectly normal morning to now descending into a black hole. It can hit you all at once, or move in slowly. It's a sinking feeling, a funk you just can't shake and might not even be able to pinpoint.

That, my friend, is a bad vibe. It may manifest itself as spontaneous anxiety or a physical need to remove yourself from a situation or just a sudden change in mood. Bad vibes can be everywhere and may attack when you least expect it. The stink eye from the woman at the checkout counter to a friend or co-worker in a terrible mood at work—you may be under siege and not even know it. A bad vibe is like carbon monoxide . . . odorless, colorless, and invisible. But it packs quite a punch. The biggest problem with a bad vibe is that, left unchecked, it can turn into a bad-vibe cycle. At that point, it's hard to see where the bad vibes are stemming from, since everything is now colored by the bad energy.

## SONIA GETS SLIMED

I gave my friend Britney a ride home one evening after partying. I was sober and more than happy to take my drunk friend home and save her the cost of an Uber. She was a bit out of my way, and the booze made her feel like talking. Britney had been in a rut lately. Her life was complicated—stuff with friends, her work, her family—and the alcohol had turned it all up to 11. And I was a captive audience.

Britney started to talk to me about our other friends—how their lives were awesome, hers not so much. It was like turning on a faucet and the handle breaking off—there was no stopping her, and one thing after another came pouring out of her mouth. Feeling sympathetic, because we all have our moments, I listened patiently. I tried to validate how she was feeling and encourage her, but it was pointless.

Britney's venting blossomed and continued. We sat in front of her house in my car, Britney alternating between laughing and crying, telling me how grateful she was that I was listening. For three hours. I felt bad that she was having a hard time, but I also wanted to shove her out of my car, hit the gas, and not look back. The larger part of me, the empath with bad boundaries (I'm working on it!), wanted to sit and hear her out.

I listened until she'd exhausted herself and had nothing else to say and then drove home in silence, really sad and hopeless. I felt bad for the way her life had unfolded, for what seemed like an impossible situation. I couldn't stop thinking about what she had told me. Her mother had just been diagnosed with breast cancer and her father's alcoholism had worsened because he didn't know how to deal. She lamented *that her brother was totally checked out and acted as though none of this was happening. She told me how her family was falling apart and she was trying to hold them all together. I crawled into bed and fell asleep, exhausted after holding the space. But I couldn't fall asleep. I tossed and turned all night, waking up with terrible nightmares. After waking up for the third time that night, I decided to send Britney loving energy, said a prayer for peace, then went back to bed. The next morning, I woke up feeling drained, as if I hadn't slept a wink. I felt utterly depressed.*

*As I got into my car to drive, I felt energetically heavy, like a small child was holding on to my neck. I didn't know if I wanted to cry or scream, so I did a little bit of both. Then I called my mom. Immediately, she could tell my energy was off.*

*I told her about how I'd driven Britney home, about how we'd sat in the car for three hours, how there were no solutions to any of Britney's problems. After a few minutes, my energy started to shift and the load started to lighten. My mom gently asked, "Is the sadness you're carrying yours?" It was an "aha" moment. Britney had held me emotionally hostage! Instead of taking care of myself by setting healthy boundaries, I'd felt obligated to sit, listen, and empathize. But she had bad-vibed me into oblivion, and I was responsible for having subjected myself to her bad vibes.*

---

The truth of the matter is that you don't have to fall victim to a secret ninja bad-vibe attack. There are many ways to escape the trap. The first step is to recognize what is happening—you're being bad-vibed. Blocking bad vibes combines some of the basic tools of using your intuition. First, be aware of yourself and your surroundings. If you are not aware of your own energy and other people's influence on it, you won't know what hit you until you walk away, shaking your head and in a terrible mood. Next, use your boundaries to establish what is a healthy energy exchange. You are in control of yourself, and that means that you have control over your reactions. The easiest way to escape bad vibes is to leave. I should have left Britney at her door earlier rather than later. Or, after the initial dumping of Britney's inebriated problems, I should have just gently said, "I'm so sorry. That must be really hard, Britney. I love you, but I have work superearly tomorrow so I can't stay. I can call you when I get off." Instead, I let myself be a dumping ground for a drunk person.

Don't trick yourself into thinking that you're being a good friend by marinating in their bad vibes. In order to take care of others, you need to be able to take care of yourself first. Otherwise, you are putting yourself in a vulnerable position where you set yourself up to be angry and resentful, which does nothing for either of you. There's an old Chinese saying that the general drinks from the well first. The general needs to serve himself in order to be of service. Otherwise, tired, depleted, and vulnerable, he is unable to help the hundreds of people counting on him for leadership. Not falling prey to unconscious behavior is self-loving, not selfish.

## CLAP BACK

If you feel like you're getting bad-vibed from your friend or co-worker, our favorite thing to do is to call the bad vibes out in a gentle way. This one time, we were receiving serious bad vibes from a waitress. She was being snippy and rude, so instead of getting annoyed with her and allowing her negative energy to spread, Sonia asked her in a gentle voice, "Are you okay?" The waitress snapped out of her funk in a heartbeat. Most people don't even realize the energy that they are putting out there. We don't know what people are going through, so a gentle reminder that their vibes are stinking up the place could be all that it takes for them to shift.

A more difficult situation is when you are trapped with a bad-vibing offender whom you can't call out, such as a boss. The best thing to do in this case is to breathe and remain aware of your own energy. One energetic technique that we use is pretending that we are in a bubble that is like a one-way mirror that allows the good energy in and reflects the bad vibes back to the offender.

Another technique is to focus on how deeply you are breathing. When we get stuck in anxiety or bad vibes, we unconsciously hold our breath or breathe shallowly. Pay attention to how your body feels and the slow inhale and exhale of your breath. Remember, you are responsible for yourself and your reaction. Do your best to not let it get to you. Or, if you can't help but be affected, go the bathroom and shake it out. Literally. Prey in the wild, if they escape getting eaten by a predator and are out of danger, will physically shake their bodies out. Make some noises with your mouth, stomp your feet, yell. Move and get back into your body and your energy. Speak it out loud. When you use your voice, you take back your power. Dance and sing at the top of your lungs. Imagine you are scaring the bad vibes away and replacing that feeling of anxiety with one of peace. If it's not dancing, then engage in yoga, running, biking, or anything physical. It brings you home, grounds you, and allows you to center yourself.

When it comes to bad vibes, you are *not* a victim. Being attacked by bad vibes is like being caught up in a case of the body snatchers. It's being displaced, energetically. As you learn to strengthen your energetic muscles and pay attention to what is going on for you, it will become easier to deflect and not become so affected.

## THE CRAZY MAKERS AND ENERGY DRAINERS

For all the wonderful friends we are blessed with, we have encountered our fair share of crazies who spread the bad vibes. They are the Regina Georges of the world, the ones who pit their friends against one another, stirring up the crazy, all while looking around and innocently asking, "What's wrong?" We like to call them frenemies.

Friends can be divided into a few camps: authentic friends, social friends, and frenemies. Frenemies talk behind your back, bring up your shortcomings, stir up drama, hide behind thinly veiled criticisms, and don't support you. Unfortunately, a lot of us keep these frenemies with us for years because of some sense of obligation. In truth, they just deplete your energy and personal resources. They are like vampires: they have the ability to "glamour" you by making you feel as though the relationship is worthwhile, when, in truth, they are draining you.

Your frenemies throw your life into upheaval. They start drama and unground you by throwing you into the hurricane that is their lives. ("Did you hear what so-and-so said about you?") They have an uncanny ability to put you in the middle of their problems, and then when you offer any sort of feedback, they turn against you, making *you* the problem. Or, every single solution that you offer can't work! If only you knew their pain! Their allure is that they're often interesting, funny, and exciting people. They may have a very sarcastic sense of humor. And at times, their shit-talking and crazy antics can be attractive, but over a long period of time, they pull you down with their negativity. They always seem to have a problem. If it's not their personal life, it's current events. If it's not current events, it's their neighbors or pets or the guy who cuts the lawn. They like to talk about how awful everything is. After hanging out with them, it is not unusual to feel physically exhausted or have bad vibes that you just cannot seem to shake.

These vampires are not necessarily bad people, but their energy and interactions are exhausting and ultimately will slow you, if not all-out stop you, from getting where you want to go. They set up roadblocks by forcing you to become stuck in low-energy frequencies such as victimhood, drama, and pettiness. They hide in plain daylight, usually going undetected, leaving you wondering, *What just happened?* Your real friends draw out the best parts of you and drive you to reach your most authentic self without drama or drain. Real friends will support and champion you without reservation.

So stake the vampires. They aren't worth the drain.

---

## *Sabrina Gets Bitten*

*My best friend growing up didn't start out as a psychic vampire. In fact, as kids, we spent fun weekends at each other's houses and vacationing together over the summer, talking about boys and supporting each other's aspirations for when we were older. We wore the same clothes, went to the same school, and told each other everything. Tina was the epitome of a best friend.*

*In middle school she was transferred to another school, and we slowly drifted apart. When Facebook was introduced into our lives in high school, we reconnected and met for coffee. When I picked her up on one summer night in Chicago I immediately noticed that something about her had changed. She was no longer the fun-loving friend I remembered. Instead, she made continuous small jabs about the fact that I had a car and commented on my clothes, my shoes, my hair, and even the vacation that I had recently been on with my family.*

*Somewhere along the way, Tina had become negative and extremely jealous of my life. Everything in her tone was laced with a feeling of I want what you have. I knew that life for her hadn't been easy. A single mom and an absent father meant that Tina's family was stressed financially; she had to worry about money in a way that I had never needed to.*

*I took her family stress into consideration when dealing with her shadow. I was so excited to reunite with my friend that I ignored how our conversations made me feel. I would leave lunch or a car ride exhausted and upset, like I had just endured a bloodletting of some sort. Worse, I found myself apologizing for and downplaying the things in my life that were working. I knew that if I were honest about my successes, she would slyly criticize me. Eventually, these small jabs added up into big cuts, and spending time with her wasn't worth it. The worst part of dealing with Tina was that she was always able to deliver the vampire traits with a smile when she was cutting me down. It wasn't obvious from the outside how draining she was on the inside.*

*I found myself steadily avoiding her phone calls. I didn't want to be around her energy because I always left feeling worse than when I arrived. I felt guilty for not wanting to be around her, but despite that, I couldn't find it within myself to answer her calls. Over time, she got the message and stopped calling. Once in a while, she would pop up and send me a text asking me how I was, and I would respond with a vague answer. I didn't even want her to know too much about me for fear that even from afar I would feel her funky jealous energy.*

*Setting up good boundaries was what kept me feeling good, and it was a choice that was good for both of us. If I had allowed the bad-vibing to continue, I would have ended up resenting her, and, ultimately, I would have been bad-vibing her right back.*

## DON'T DRINK THE POISON

Recently we were in an airport traveling to a workshop together and watched a man knock over an elderly woman during the boarding process because he wanted to be the first person on the airplane. As all the other passengers rushed to help the woman, the man seemed genuinely surprised that anyone would take offense at his behavior. When we get stressed out (such as in line at the airport or under duress for an upcoming deadline), our brains disconnect from something called the frontal cortex. When this disconnect happens, we end up acting in insensitive, rude, obtuse, unconscious, or just purposefully inflammatory ways because we are disconnected from the more evolved parts of our human consciousness.

Dealing with others when they are in this mental state is exhausting and will usually end up creating an equal reaction in your own body if you're not paying attention. Have you ever gotten blindsided with angry energy by a friend or family member, just to turn around and unload that same energy on to someone else? We know we've been guilty of it from time to time. Even by accident, all that funky energy will try to find an outlet, and dealing with someone's shitty energy will mean learning how to get rid of it without throwing it off you and onto some unsuspecting victim.

We all handle things in different ways. Some choose to scream and shout, while others shut down, preferring to ignore the conflict in hopes that it will go away. In our family, when we start fights with each other or hurt each other's feelings, we say to one another, "Did you poop in the pool?" It's a quick way to point out someone's made a mistake and they need to clean it up. We're humans, we will make thousands of mistakes—it's called learning. But if we make a mistake, we have to clean it up. And if someone else makes a mistake, it's important to let them know so they have an opportunity to clean it up. If we don't let people correct their mistakes, it's easy to start telling stories, stay angry, and let that anger turn into resentment. Anger can be seductive; it allows us to feel in control. When used in a healthy way, it communicates boundaries, as in, "Hey, don't do that. That's not okay." But if we get addicted to anger, we get resentful. Resentment allows you to feel justified and empowered in your feelings of anger and hurt. But in truth it holds you back and taints your own well, drying up your resources of forgiveness and goodwill.

Resentment can feel like a badge of honor, but that's just your ego faking you out. Our resentments can provide us with important clues on where we don't feel witnessed or seen, or where we have overgiven or been hurt. It's a place where we don't want to let go or forgive. Sometimes, if we forgive someone, it can feel like we've released that person from any responsibility and that what they did to us is okay. But if we don't forgive, we hold on to resentment. Resentment is like a hungry little gremlin that feeds on negativity; it finds any opportunity to remind you that your anger is justified. And that little gremlin makes us think that he's not affecting our relationships, but he is. It might manifest in different ways, like being passive-aggressive or feeling injured at any slight. The gremlin may make us feel temporarily better, but what we're really doing is hurting each other and feeding our gremlins so they grow and grow until our tiny gremlins are giant monsters that wipe out all of our compassion.

In order to not become entranced by resentment, we first need to get in touch with how we feel. What is under the anger? A lot of times, our feelings were hurt and we feel bad. We get focused on what someone did instead of how it made us feel.

If we decide to be really honest about how we feel and meet our hurt feelings with self-compassion, we start to open doors to moving the energy. When we're feeling hurt and resentful, we have to be kind to ourselves first and foremost. Without this, it can make healing conversations impossible. If we share how another person's actions made us feel and we're curious about how *they* feel, we build a bridge and create an honest and open dialogue. When we can talk about it and hear one another, we can genuinely forgive and move the energy.

Clearing resentments isn't easy. In some cases, if people are really unhealthy or a relationship is really toxic, it's unsafe to open these doors. We have to be compassionate with ourselves, and when we're ready, we can find that compassion for the person who has hurt us. Until we address and heal our hurt, we can't access that compassion or forgiveness for someone else. We can't do a spiritual bypass. We have to move the energy and find safe people to talk to.

Feel your feelings, cry, yell, get mad. All of the above are important. Until you feel your feelings and have compassion for yourself, you won't let go. And if it's really bad, we suggest finding a therapist who can help you sort through it. Your feelings have to be acknowledged and recognized as valid, even if there's a sprinkle of crazy in there. Emotions aren't logical. If you're feeling resentful for whatever reason, own it, find a way to express it in a nondestructive way, and forgive, so you don't have to carry around all that heaviness.

## SETTING UP GOOD BOUNDARIES

Most of us do our best with what we have. We learn from our families how to be in the world. It would be great if everyone were loving, kind, and compassionate, but the truth of the matter is that people are a bit unpredictable. When you get hooked into others as your source of happiness, it's like getting on the *Titanic*: you're going down. Predicating your own happiness on the attitude of people around you isn't going to work. We have a saying— "Stay in your own lane." What does that mean? It means that you need to take care of yourself and not get energetically hooked.

Know what your boundaries are. What is a boundary? A boundary is "something that indicates or fixes a limit or extent." In terms of relationships, a boundary is your personal line or limit, a "Go no further" sign that keeps the bad vibes out. It says, *this* is okay and *that* is not okay. These are not walls—boundaries don't keep people out. They keep you and the people you love safe because you create relationships that are emotionally healthy for you.

Often, we aren't even aware of our boundaries until someone has crossed them. Maybe you've had the experience where someone asks you for a favor but you don't really want to do it. You ignore yourself and do it anyway, later feeling resentful of that person. Or maybe it's a friend or co-worker who keeps asking you for more and more favors and you keep doing them, all the while keeping a secret tally. You might think, *I've done so much for you, and what have you ever done for me?*

How do we have compassion and take care of ourselves in the face of difficult encounters? First, we need to separate the ego from the Spirit. As discussed, we develop our ego in order to protect ourselves from this wide world of crazy. But our Spirits are that pure, loving wonderful presence that exists within each of us. So we love the Spirits of those who challenge us and we learn how to cultivate compassion for their egos. Often, when people are really unhealthy, they have gone through trauma and have no tools to deal. So we can have compassion for them, but that doesn't mean we have to take care of them.

Caretaking is putting aside your needs and emotional well-being in order to take care of someone else. In reality, it's a form of control. When we caretake, the other person's emotions overwhelm us, and we try and calm them down so we feel better. Caretaking is very different from being a good friend. Remember my friend Britney? Caretaking. So when you are faced with a person who challenges your boundaries, ask yourself, *Do I want to do this? Does this take care of me?* If you're in real deep, sometimes it can be difficult to get in touch with what you need. Start by checking in with how you *feel*. Does it feel good? Why or why not? Are you giving too much?

When we learn to set boundaries, it's a new practice, just like tuning in to your intuition. It's okay to be a beginner. Your boundaries let people know what works for you and what doesn't, and what the consequences are if they don't respect your boundary. Healthy boundaries are communicated in a clear and grounded way. It's not a punishment or a way to manipulate—it allows you to let people know what you expect of them, what you're going to allow and what you're not. For example, let's say you have a friend who gets stupid drunk every time you go out. Every time they get blackout drunk, maybe they put you in unsafe situations, or you end up having to take care of them and make sure they get home safe. This is where you put up a boundary at a neutral time—not while you're pregaming at your friend's house, or after ordering a few drinks, but while you're getting lunch. You can say something like this:

"I love you, but when you get blackout drunk, it's not fun. If we go out, you can't get wasted, and if you do, then we need to hang out during the day. I feel angry when I constantly have to take care of you because it makes me responsible for you. I'm not judging you, but this is something I need to take care of me and our friendship."

Congratulations! You just set a boundary. Now, this part is key: when you set a boundary, you need to be able to follow through. It's not a threat, but just a clear line. If you go out and they get scary wasted, then your part is to follow through and not go out with them next time they invite you. If they ask you why, be up front. Your job is to not put yourself in a vulnerable position and to hold up your end of the bargain.

When we set up boundaries, we need to get neutral beforehand. Especially if it's an uncomfortable boundary, people will try and hook you into their emotions as a way to get you to relinquish the limits you've set. Although it's uncomfortable in the moment and maybe even a little while afterward, they will learn that you mean what you say. The two of you have just entered into a contract that if x happens, then y will happen. It's not personal, just what you need to do to take care of yourself. Since this is a new practice, you're going to make mistakes. That is okay. In the words of Aaliyah, you need to dust yourself off, and you need to try again.

The thing about boundaries is that they aren't set in stone. The boundary that works for today might shift and change and be different down the road. The most important part is to be in touch with your feelings. The way we feel is our personal litmus test for which boundaries work and which ones don't.

We can have compassion for people, for their struggles, but we need to also have compassion for ourselves. Our boundaries empower us and allow us to not get hooked into other people's drama. They are our way of being self-loving, taking personal responsibility for our own happiness.

---

### Will You Watch My Cat?

*I had a client recently who called me and told me that her boss, and her entire work environment for that matter, was comprised of vampires. She noted that every time she entered her office, she would literally want to fall asleep. It was as though someone had given her an Ambien. I explained that this was in fact a normal reaction for a lot of sensitive people around vampires or in vampire–inhabited environments. They're exhausting!*

*She worked at a law office that specialized in divorce. All the clients were in trauma over the deaths of their marriages, and people in trauma tend to not care how they're affecting* others. Now add money and child custody to the equation, and you have an intense environment.

A recent graduate from law school, Caitlyn was still adjusting to the working world, and because she was the new kid on the block, every single one of her co-workers asked her to do things that were absolutely not her job. Could she get coffee? Could she stay late to make copies? Would she deal with the backed-up toilets in the men's room? Could she babysit her boss's cat over the holiday weekend even though she was devastatingly allergic and needed to pop Benadryl like PEZ candy in the cat's presence?

All this is to say that Caitlyn needed her job and didn't want to quit, so we came up with a game plan to deal with the energy suck. Before entering the office, she would check in with her own energy. Was she tired? Had she slept and eaten enough? Was she grounded in herself? "Literally imagine yourself as the Empire State Building before walking into the office," I suggested. "Be a strong building rooted in the ground in the midst of chaos."

For the first few days, Caitlyn noticed that she was able to hold herself in this space until around lunchtime, and then the phone ringing and the constant demands would wear her down.

"All right. So we know that you're less susceptible to the vampire energy when you take care of yourself, correct?" I asked.

"Correct," Caitlyn answered.

"Do you go out to lunch?" I asked.

"Not really. I usually just down a PowerBar and a coffee at my desk. Technically speaking, we can leave for 30 minutes, but I don't. I'm afraid of how they'll react or the pile of requests on my desk when I get back. Sometimes I am even afraid to pee."

"All right. Let's try an experiment. Instead of sitting at your desk, try going out to your car for fifteen minutes of that lunch-break time and let them know that they can text you if they need you. Don't tell them where you're going, but that if they need you, you're not far."

The next week when Caitlyn called me, she was a changed woman. Not only was it working and she was no longer drained to the bone, but not one of her colleagues had asked her to do anything above and beyond her job description for the entire week. By putting up a boundary, Caitlyn got her co-workers to see her as a person, one who was able to get up from her desk and take care of herself. She started bringing her walking shoes with her to work and going for a reinvigorating walk before returning to her desk.

The best part was that her lunch break had changed the dynamics in the office. More of her colleagues were leaving for a break in the day, and because of this, everyone was having a much happier and more productive afternoon. Caitlyn had unintentionally created a better work environment for everyone, and the only thing her boss asked her was if she had gotten a haircut. (She hadn't. Her boss could just feel that something in Caitlyn had changed.)

---

We are only truly susceptible to bad vibes and vampires if we consistently allow them in instead of putting up a boundary.

The thing with vampires, both in fiction and in real life, is that the vampire can't get in if we don't invite them. Sometimes that means saying, "Yeah, I'm not available to babysit your cat, whom I am extremely allergic to." Or, "No, I can't sit here for hours while you dump your drunken emotional crap on me." It's having self-esteem enough to know that you can say *no* to what doesn't work for you and *yes* to what does. It's acknowledging the effect that others have and knowing that when you leave the room on your knees from exhaustion every single time you deal with a particular person, something may, in fact, be off in your dynamic, and you have to take action to correct the imbalance.

We've found that when we're the dumping ground for the bad vibes of other people, it actually doesn't help anyone. By not participating, we can instead positively influence another person. It's like giving an untrained dog a boundary not to bite you and crap all over your living room while you watch. It's saying, "No, you can't do those things. I am not okay with this." You don't hurt the dog—he doesn't know better. You just train him.

## HELP YOURSELF

- Be aware of yourself and your own energy. You will be less susceptible to bad-vibe sneak attacks.

- Remove yourself from the situation. If you can't remove yourself, pretend that you're in the middle of a one-way mirror ball. Good energy is allowed to freely pass in between the mirror, but bad vibes are reflected back.

- Practice setting your boundaries—and keeping them!

- If you don't know what boundaries you need to set, get out a journal and think about the people in your life and have a pretend conversation with them. What would you say if they were willing to obey any boundary you would set?

- Check in with your feeling body. How do you feel? Keep checking in with yourself. If you can't discern your feelings, start writing down what you're grateful for. The gratitude journal will help you check back in with yourself.

- Continually check in with your boundaries as they shift and change. What worked for you last year may not be okay now!

- If you are attacked by a bad vibe and can't shake it, take a bath, move your body, or get back into your own energy field.

- Make sure your relationships uplift you. Don't subject yourself to assholes because you think you don't deserve better. You do.

CHAPTER 6

# FILLING
# THE VOID

## WHAT MONEY CAN'T BUY

From the cradle, our generation has been constantly flooded with images, symbols, and subconscious conditioning. These messages are meant to convince us that products, clothes, or even food are what we need to feel happy. Remember how happy the kids were in the Sunny D commercial? Or the kids with the toys in the commercials that played during our Saturday-morning cartoons? The companies that were trying to sell us happiness have succeeded. Our generation consumes more on a daily basis than any generation in history. We devour the Internet, coffee, lunch, television, music, pop culture, the news—usually all before we hit our desks for work. (Our own car ride this morning included all of the above.)

There is a quote that often bubbles up on social media that says, "Not all who wander are lost." This idea is romantic, but in reality we as a generation have no idea where we're going and are more stressed about it than we're willing to let on. Our peers travel from party to party, from store to store, from relationship to relationship, trying to fill the void they feel when they lay their heads down on their pillows at night.

In a way, we are guinea pigs. The world is radically different from the one we inherited from our parents. Do you ever sit on the couch and watch TV while you text, simultaneously checking Facebook or Snapchat? We do. It's become second nature to have constant stimuli and zone out. Because we're the first wave of kids who grew up with the Internet, we have become accustomed to constantly being entertained and sold "happiness." Look at advertisements—most of the time we aren't even being peddled a product but an experience—it's not a car, it's your ticket to beautiful women fawning all over you. It's not just an outfit but validation, acceptance, being cool. The power of the Internet has graced us with access to anything and everything that we could possibly desire, delivered to our doorstep. Ten years ago, our attention span was 12 minutes long; now the average attention span is 5 seconds, just like a goldfish. Holy crap! Western culture has indoctrinated our generation from the start to want the newest, best, and most exciting thing. *Not* being marketed and sold to no longer exists. There is product placement in TV shows, music videos, on Instagram, Facebook—literally *everywhere* you look.

We have been brainwashed into thinking that money can buy happiness. But it doesn't. There was a study created by a professor from Northwestern and a professor from the University of Massachusetts comparing happiness of people who become paralyzed in traumatic accidents and those who win big in the lottery. The results found that over time, people who win the lottery and people who become paralyzed in traumatic accidents are equally as happy. If you break that down, even though you may have won the lottery, after a while you become accustomed to your new wealth, and your happiness might even decrease because nothing will ever compare to winning the lottery. People who suffer in traumatic accidents struggle at first, but as they grow accustomed to their new way of life, they become happier and their everyday life gets better.

Let's be brutally honest. We are the instant generation; we want what we want and we want it now. It's 3 A.M. and you need a beaded tunic by tomorrow? Done. Goat's milk from China? Absolutely. But, deep down, we want more—more authenticity, more connection. Our constant distraction disconnects us from our Spirits, and when we have a rare moment of quiet, we feel empty. Our instant, need-it-now world has made it so that we have become separated from the *real* world—and we feel that separation acutely even as we wait for the new purchase, or the bottle of vodka, or the cupcake to fill us up. The problem is, feeling happy and connected to your heart will never come from an outside source.

Let's flip the script. Happiness, a real sense of well-being, is in reality just a breath away.

If you focus on feeling connected and centered on the inside, enjoying all that life has to offer on the outside becomes easy. You'll know what you need. (Are you sensing a theme here?) You'll know what you want. Your heart will tell you. This approach will balance your life *and* your bank account. Happiness is earned. It's earned by being available to yourself enough to build your life around what truly feeds your heart.

---

### Sabrina Hates Santa Claus

*Recently, I was walking through the mall on the hunt for a new pair of Joe's skinny jeans. Because of my post-Thanksgiving timing, Christmas sales had drawn all of the suburban shoppers to Chicago, and navigating the downtown Nordstrom turned into a serious game of Frogger.*

*No one was walking fast enough for me. The people around me seemed to be actually moving in slow motion. Families stopped in large groups, all at once, and blocked the passageways completely. Why? Because at the other end of the mall sat Santa Claus. Babies, toddlers, stressed-out parents, and even Santa's elves had created an intense road-block. I seethed to myself,* I really hate you, Santa Claus. I really fucking hate you.

*Ridiculous, right? In retrospect, I was overtired from teaching six weekends in a row. I hadn't been taking care of my happiness, my needs, or even my basics, and it manifested in that moment I seriously considered cursing Santa Claus, out loud, at Nordstrom. I was angry at all of these people, who just seemed so in my way. But it really had nothing to do with the strollers or Santa's elves. I was the one with a terrible attitude and an agenda, and if I had only slowed down, taken a good, deep breath, and enjoyed the holiday spirit around me, I might have not made life so hard on myself.*

*My inner void was coloring everything around me. I know how seductive it is to slip into a vicious cycle of negative thoughts and behaviors. It's easy to become the crazy person with a chip on your shoulder if you're not looking out for your own energy, or worse, trying to get your needs met in all wrong places. Did I mention I was at Nordstrom that day to buy yet another pair of jeans I absolutely didn't need?*

*I, among the teeming holiday shoppers, was trying to fill my void in vain. The justification usually goes something like this:* This top will make me feel better about the fact that the guy I'm interested in hasn't called me back. Or, I've been working so hard, it's fine for me to blow my paycheck on this new purse.

*My mind tells me that if I spend money on myself I will feel better. I usually hit the hard wall of reality, though, after the initial endorphin rush of my new purchase wears off, and I am back to exactly where I started emotionally. The purchase never does the emotional job I want it to. Jeans don't call you back either.*

*Trying to find happiness through any external force or object only leads to disappointment. I am as much as victim to this as any other 20-something in the world. And this is not to devalue beautiful things or fabulous experiences but just to say that they're the cherry on top of the cake, not the cake itself.*

---

## AIN'T NO PARTY HERE

We're all for a good party. We both love to dance, sing, and get silly, and we're usually down to go out. We both love to get dressed up and enjoy throwing back a few cocktails to a thumping bass at a sweaty club. We have, however, identified an epidemic of our peers looking for happiness in the club.

In our early 20s we had a friend named Adela who would whip herself up into a near frenzy about "going out." She would spend her workweek longing for the weekend. Once the weekend did roll around, she would drink to excess, overspend on bottles of alcohol, and usually end up in bed with someone she hadn't known for more than a couple of hours.

Adela would inevitably call Sunday morning, head throbbing, bloated and regretful of all the "stupid choices" she had made the night before. But come Wednesday, without fail, the itch to "go out" would begin again. She would get intense talking about the "release I absolutely need from partying."

Slowly, Adela's obsessive party-girl personality drove a wedge between us. It was too much to try and keep up with her, and there was *never* a happy ending to any of her club stories. The whole thing was a downer, and any suggestion that she might be looking for happiness in the wrong place was met with defensiveness and defiance. The last straw: she called Sabrina an "annoying old lady" because she didn't want to go to a warehouse rave on a ridiculously cold Chicago winter night.

A club or bar is an empty place if you're looking for it to fill up your happiness tank. Stromae, Belgium DJ and European superstar, said it well: "We try to sell happiness in clubs, but you can't. Because life is life, and even if you try to hide it, you can read on different faces that they have problems."

He's right. Think of every song on the radio right now that is about clubbing. How in the world are we supposed to live up to all that hype? The amount of pressure to have a good time and Instagram or Snapchat it is so high that anything less than a perfect, glamorous, raucous evening ends up feeling like New Year's Eve: never as good as it's supposed to be.

We've learned that you can have fun at the club if you've got fun already in your heart—when you're not looking for anyone to make you feel beautiful, when you're not drinking to numb your emotions. (Refresher—they'll still surface one way or another!) But you can't go there to get your core happiness needs met. It won't happen. Because, just like Adela, you will end up lower and more miserable than where you started. The club without a happy heart is the perfect incubator for actual sadness.

We have certain festivals, DJs, and clubbing experiences that we look forward to attending all year, like Burning Man, Electric Forest, or Lollapalooza. And if we're in a good space, it's our favorite time of year. What's interesting is that many in our generation don't go to church like the generations before us on the weekends. We *pray* we don't miss out on the party. For many of us, partying has become our generation's religion. Add the constant public documentation of our lives, and voilà: stress. But if you're going out looking to fill an empty hole in your life, chances are you're going to hit the floor, not feel the bass, hard.

## WE CAN'T STOP EATING THE CHOCOLATE

We love to feed the soul with a homemade batch of chocolate chip cookies or a rich beef stew on a cold winter day. When food is in its proper place, being used to nourish our bodies and even explore our creativity or adventurous selves, it's a wonderful way to connect to our hearts.

This isn't the type of food we are talking about here. We've all been there—using food as medicine to mend our broken or depleted hearts, having a sweet treat as a reward for a challenging day. In fact, we both reach for a bar of dark chocolate when we're upset. We keep it stocked in the fridge just in case we need a feel-good pick-me-up. Reaching for comfort food isn't necessarily a problem. It only becomes damaging when overeating is compounded by feelings of guilt plus whatever pain you're trying to soothe in the first place.

If your only go-to when you're stressed, tired, drained, upset, angry, or bored is food, overeating has become a problem. Using food as an emotional habit or distraction doesn't feed the hole. It just feeds your stomach temporarily.

We had a client who would yo-yo diet. He would go back and forth between extreme overeating and extreme dieting. He would limit his food for a few weeks, and then turn around and completely rebel against his own control and overconsume. This left him exhausted, poorly nourished, and mostly feeling shitty about himself and his body. His love/hate relationship with food occupied his time and his energies. Josh knew his eating habits weren't healthy, but he never stopped to check in with his Spirit about the effect that this was having on him.

"Food makes me feel completely out of control," Josh said. "I eat when I'm stressed; I don't eat when I'm stressed. I use food to distract myself and I use food to make myself feel better. I use food to feed things that food can't feed." He hit it right on the head. The food wasn't going to help him ultimately feel better. Instead, it distracted him from being able to focus on what was really draining him.

So we came up with a system. Instead of going on a "diet," Josh would keep a journal, and every time before he sat down to eat anything he would write about his emotional state first. *How are you feeling? What's on your mind?* These were Josh's prompts.

He realized early on that he would fall prey to disordered eating when he was stressed and overwhelmed. When he was grounded, he ate consciously. He was likely to overindulge at night when he was bored or lonely. He ate mindfully when he was with others, and less so when he was alone. This was all valuable information. Now that Josh knew his patterns, we implemented a system where he would check in with himself before eating. Slowing down and raising his awareness shifted how he used food. It also allowed him to be more compassionate with himself when he overdid it.

Josh still struggles on some days. This by no means was the end of his love/hate relationship with food. However, it did shift his approach to eating. He checks in more often and is able to make better choices.

## OKAY, GUYS, I'M BROKE AND HUNGOVER. NOW WHAT?

How do you break your bad habits? Well, first thing's first. When the impulse to overdrink or overshop or over-anything comes up, it's because you need something deeper. It's a technique for temporary relief or distraction. It's a Band-Aid over a bullet wound.

But when we allow ourselves a moment of quiet to listen to ourselves, we can hear what it is we *really need*. We have everything we need to make us happy already, no matter the circumstance. That might sound crazy, but it's true. In real life, shit happens and always will happen. There is no pause button, nor is happiness a destination. A lot of us believe that happiness is waiting for us once the circumstances align. It's simply not true.

Life is stressful. If you're constantly waiting to arrive, you'll always look back to those times "when everything was great" and realize that you didn't even notice that it was good. You'll forget that happiness starts right now *despite* all the shit going on around you. When you are connected to your Spirit first and foremost, you know what you need. This is huge. We say it over and over because it's just that important. It's a stupidly simple notion, but when you feed your Spirit by giving yourself those things that take care of you, your happiness increases tenfold.

Unhappy? Tune in to your intuition and ask *why*. The funny thing is that we like to play dumb and pretend we have no idea. But you know exactly what isn't working—and you can change it. Get quiet. Put down your phone, computer, iPad, whatever, and just take a few minutes and get in touch with how you feel. It may be helpful to keep a small journal. Ask yourself nonjudgmentally: *What am I trying to accomplish with this* [food, alcohol, shopping, risky sex]? Mark down the factors at play and be curious about why you're acting out in the way you are. If you're not sure if you're acting out or just having fun, ask yourself if you feel guilty. If you feel bad about what you're doing and you do it again and again, it's time to check yourself.

If you can breathe and check in with yourself, in that place there's a small voice that'll tell you what's really going on. This is the voice of your heart, and it might suggest that what you need is big or small. It might say you need a hug, or it might tell you that you're in the wrong job or with the wrong person. It might feel scary to listen to this voice because it seems easier to ignore it and cover it up with stuff like food or alcohol. But the truth is, this inner voice is your inner teacher. It's trying to wake you up to something, and it's up to you to listen. But, remember, you always have a choice. We see a lot of people not listening to their intuition because the implication is that if they really hear it, and acknowledge what it's saying, they'll have to do whatever it suggests. Not necessarily. First, you listen. Then, you take action. Or don't. That part is up to you.

)(

Our friend Alexandra, with her whimsical disposition and pixie haircut, is the quintessential preschool teacher and free spirit. Recently, Alexandra moved into her own studio apartment in Harlem. The space was small and often noisy, but it was all hers. She told us about how she had just purchased a movie projector off of Craigslist from an old Israeli man. She moved her furniture and watched French films on the entire wall of her tiny apartment, making herself a scrumptious meal for one. She could relax at the end of the day in peace and quiet. She had found her own identity in the small space, a real sense of self, and it was her safe place to get quiet and just be. For the first time, she was really taking care of herself, and in that place of self-care, she started to feel happy.

"I was scared that I wouldn't be able to afford the rent when I first moved in, since it was more expensive than living with a roommate. But the reality is, I'm actually saving money now that I live alone." She tucked her hair behind her ears and smiled. "I used to say to myself, 'I'll buy this shirt; that will make me happy.' I used to spend money to try and feel happy. Now, in my own space with my own door to close, I am just getting to know myself. I don't need the shirt anymore, and I have more money. I'm just naturally happier." Alexandra addressed her own core needs, and the over-doing fixed itself.

So now the question becomes, what really takes care of your needs? For us, it's kickboxing, listening to music, singing, making home-cooked meals, laughing with friends, doing our counseling work, writing this book. All of these activities fill us up and bring us joy. We sit with our own inner voice regularly and recognize our shitty energy, or our own black holes when we get down in the dumps. We do our best not to throw money at the holes or stuff the holes down deeper with distractions.

Acknowledging our needs and then fulfilling them is the equation that will actually lead you on the path toward happiness. If you check in and recognize what *does* make you happy, and really own what truthfully *doesn't*, you'll avoid the pitfalls of trying to find happiness at the bottom of the wine bottle, with a maxed-out credit card, or in the bed of a stranger. As cliché as it may sound, happiness starts by filling yourself up with what you love about yourself and about life, and then anything you do from there will only make the experience of being here that much better.

## HELP YOURSELF

- Get quiet. You don't need to meditate for an hour every day, but take a few minutes when you wake up and check in with how you feel. Ask yourself, *What do I need?*

- Think of the last time you were last triggered to fill a void, and ask yourself why. Is it that you weren't getting enough sleep? Did you have an argument with a friend? Triggers are a great way to unearth what it is you need if you look under your initial reaction.

- Keep a small Moleskine journal and a great writing pen with you at all times. When you find yourself overdoing, ask the questions: *What am I trying to accomplish? What do I need?* Be available to the answers. Write them down.

- Put down your phone and learn to be here now. Pay attention to what is going on around you.

- Get a good crew and support system! No man is an island. Talk it out.

- Slow down. We're trained to constantly be on to the next thing, but the old saying "Stop and smell the roses" holds true.

- Cultivate a meditation practice. Meditation really just means listening. Become a good listener and allow your heart to speak.

CHAPTER 7

# CHECK YOURSELF BEFORE YOU WRECK YOURSELF: BEING RIGHT, RESENTMENT, AND BULLSHIT

## HOW DO YOU SHOW UP?

We affect one another, plain and simple. As we're on this learning journey (hello, life!) and becoming more aware, we have to be responsible for how we show up—and the energy we put out into the world. So we need to be sure to clean up our own shit. It's not fun. No one volunteers to clean the litter box. Ever had a bad day and been a dick to your best friend? We have. We live insanely stressful lives. We are overbooked, overscheduled, and overstimulated, and we feel it. Sometimes, we let our worst emotions drive the car, and they can be terrible drivers. If you're feeling overextended, it shows up in a lot of different ways: anger, defensiveness, resentment. We're not saying that these emotions are "bad," but they are huge signals that we need pay attention, take a time-out, and give ourselves some self-care because we're suffering from a case of bad vibes. Let's be real: it's impossible to have a great attitude each and every day, but you can still be thoughtful about where you're at so you don't slime everyone around you.

We don't always pay attention to how we show up in our day-to-day and affect others. The way that we show up sets a certain tone. Our energy is powerful. Ever been around someone in a bad mood and you can just feel it? Like that. Just like a first impression, our vibes say more about us than we sometimes realize. Are you the person who people are happy to see, or are you the one they run away from? If you suspect you may often be the latter, let's ask some questions: Is every single boss you have a nightmare? Are all your roommates assholes? Are you always surrounded by drama? If you answer yes to all these questions, we're going to have to go ahead and tell you to check yourself because you might need a vibe adjustment.

Sometimes it isn't you who is sliming everyone around you. But on those days when everything pisses you off and your bullshit is off the charts, know that you get what you give—and that includes your vibe.

---

## SONIA'S NOT RIGHT—OR WRONG

*When I was dating my ex-boyfriend—let's go ahead and call him Bob—we would battle over who was right from topics that ranged from who said what a week ago to where to eat dinner. It would be an all-out bloodbath. When I ended up the victor, with Bob in submission, relinquishing the title of "right," I felt great . . . for a little while. I would get high on it. Oh, I'm right, he's wrong, he finally admitted it. After the adrenaline wore off, we would sit in our angry separate corners—me resenting having to battle and him hating to feel wrong. It did nothing to bring us together but instead left us empty and resentful. Neither of us felt like the other understood where we were coming from, nor did we feel validated.*

*I learned that being right wasn't the sweet victory I wanted it to be. My need to win made it harder to hear what he was saying or understand what he was needing from me. I wouldn't appreciate what his actual grievance was and instead just fought, telling him that he didn't understand me. It was like being trapped in quicksand. The more we struggled to convince each other of our points of view, the deeper we got into our argument.*

*One day, I was lamenting to my girlfriends for the millionth time how Bob had failed me. These friends, understandably, had by this point started to hate him after constantly hearing me bitch about what a jerk he was. However, instead of jumping on the "he's a jerk" bandwagon, absurdly, now all I wanted to do was defend him. He wasn't a bad guy. Bob was a wonderful person, and in the midst of all our bickering, I had forgotten to look past my ego and remember who he was. The more married I was to my perspective, the more it had polarized us. He was bad, I was good. He was wrong, I was right. Not only was my commitment to being right ruining our relationship, but I was creating a new reality for everyone who loved me.*

*After a particularly nasty fight, I decided that my current tactics weren't working. I was going to put down my battle-ax, wave my white flag, and try to understand where he was coming from. I was going to give up being "right." I won't lie: it was hard. He pushed every single button I had. I bit my tongue. I squirmed. I had to take deep breaths and count to 10. I left the room for a time-out, as I could feel my blood pressure mounting. I decided to focus on hearing him, and everything shifted.*

*Although it didn't work out in the end (we just weren't a good fit for each other), the lesson to let go of "being right" was a huge gift for which I am still so grateful to have learned.*

---

Being right is great food for the ego, but it disconnects us from each other, from our Spirits, and it definitely puts out a bad vibe. Being right is temporarily awesome, but in reality, it's a lonely experience. It's a futile exercise in control, because the fact remains—we can't control someone else's subjective experience.

So if being right isn't as satisfying as we think it is, why do we fight to the death? Many of us have learned from the time we were small that being "wrong" is shameful. When we're wrong, we're dumb. We're in a culture where admitting we're wrong is considered a weakness. But we're human, so we will definitely fuck up from time to time. Instead of using those times when we make mistakes as a time to be nice to ourselves because we're learning, we have believed that we need to defend our honor to the death.

When we shut down the "being right" thing and instead try to openly communicate and understand one another, everything softens. At the end of the day, we want to be *heard*, understood, validated. We want to feel like people get us and where we're coming from. Validation isn't about one person being right or wrong. It's about feeling like our feelings are understood. Our emotions are an intrinsic part of who we are, and telling someone that what they are feeling is wrong invalidates their experience and tells them that something with *them* is wrong. No one's feelings are wrong. When someone hurts your feelings, you're not wrong for feeling that way. For example, when a friend accidentally hurts your feelings—let's say they forgot to include you on a group outing—and instead of apologizing, they tell you that you're overreacting, it just fills you with more hurt and upset. What was a misunderstanding or an oversight might escalate the bad feelings. What you want is for your friend to say, "Hey, I wasn't trying to not include you, but I totally get that you have hurt feelings. I'm sorry. I love you."

When our feelings are validated ("I get why you feel that way"), we can genuinely move on. But, if we get into a battle royale about who is "right" in the situation, we get into trouble. What are we really arguing about then? Many times, we argue about "facts," but since each person's experience is subjective, the facts vary from person to person. If you've ever taken Psych 101, there's a whole thing on the credibility of eyewitness testimony and how we remember things. It's not reliable. So when we fight about "facts," it's kind of pointless. It becomes a battle of pride, and nobody really "wins."

Negative emotions don't simply go away. Wouldn't it be nice if they did? But they don't, and if we don't address them, they leak into everything, especially the important relationships in our lives. You can run, but you can't hide. We've tried. The shit of life, all those hard experiences and uncomfortable stuff, if unaddressed, will find a way into the world, so dealing with it is fundamental in living an empowered life. When we deal with stuff head on, it doesn't sneak up and trap us.

This is where the *c* word comes in. Say it with me now: compassion. We keep coming back to it, but we first need to have compassion for ourselves and our injuries. Instead of trying to think our way around an issue, argue, or validate our position, if we drop in and genuinely are kind and comforting to ourselves, we start to soften. We don't have to be at war anymore. Once we can start being compassionate and *feeling* that compassion, we can start to extend those feelings to others and ourselves. We can relax enough to get into the other person's head. We can see that maybe they got scared or felt judged—and we can imagine their point of view.

When we get triggered, our ego is our first line of defense. It thinks, *I'm not safe—screw this!* It puts distance between us and a loved one as a way to protect us from getting hurt. This isn't necessarily a bad thing, but our egos have a great ability to self-select out. The injury can be addictive, and if we fall under that spell, it puts us on a false pedestal of being "better than" or "victimized," and to be honest, they're both isolating and boring. But if we allow ourselves to feel and express our feelings, look at the root of them, offer compassion to ourselves, and try to understand each other, we genuinely forgive and let it go.

That said, having compassion doesn't mean being a doormat or putting yourself in abusive situations. This is where your boundaries come in. Boundaries are what keep you safe and are informed by your needs. If you're in touch with what you need and what your true *yes* and *no* are, you can take responsibility for your part, no matter who you're with.

## NEVER LEAVE THE HOUSE WITHOUT YOUR BULLSHIT METER

Being a young person is all about making mistakes and learning from them. We love mistakes. But we also get to decide what kind of person we are going to be. Are you going to be *that* guy or the wonderful person you know you are? We have to acknowl-edge that the way we live our lives and conduct ourselves is our responsibility. There's an epidemic of bullshittiness that is infect-ing our generation. Within our consumer culture, selfie over-load and our YOLO attitude, there has been a shift toward "just not giving a fuck." From one angle, this is empowering, but from another, it's the worst.

The kind of bullshit that we are talking about has many dif-ferent faces.

It might look like dishonesty. Do you lie when you're uncom-fortable or shift blame to someone else when you've made a mis-take? It might look like being two-faced, or using manipulation to get ahead, with friends or at a job or in a relationship. It may look like you're setting up unrealistic expectations for yourself or others, and then getting angry when you or someone else aren't "perfect." Or you might be gossiping about other people. Do you talk shit to build yourself up? Do you throw others under the bus when they're not around? Your bullshit may be jerking others around emotionally or creating drama for drama's sake.

Or maybe you're the kind of bullshitter who's more under-cover. Our favorite bullshit line we hear is when people answer a question with a thoughtless "I don't know." Do you really not know? Or is it easier to *pretend* you don't, so you don't have to make a decision? We've all got our baggage, our shadows, our not-so-nice parts that are just plain human. But we need to keep our shit in check.

When people are bullshitty, it's usually just a cover-up for insecurity, an overcompensation in order to make up for per-ceived shortcomings. We live our lives via social media, and it allows us to disconnect from our authentic selves and become hypnotized by what is "cool." Instead of being interested, we want to be *interesting*, further creating this cycle of self-indulgence.

So how willing are you to deny your bullshit? How willing are you to let it run your life? As our godmother Luann used to say, "What you don't own, owns you."

That is, if you're not willing to look at it, chances are that's because you're making powerful choices from bullshit places.

---

## This Party Is Bullshit!

*Sonia and I attended a birthday dinner party for our old friend Chris. Walking into the house that night, we could just feel that the energy was off. The smiles were in place, the champagne was flowing, and the music was loud—but everyone was acting tense. It looked like a party! Why didn't it feel like one? The faint smell of bullshit seemed to be wafting over the room from somewhere.*

*A couple of minutes into the party, we turned to each other and identified the perpetrator: Chris's girlfriend, Megan. She was sitting in the corner of the room on a small wooden stool. Arms folded, her body kicked back. She was glaring at the floor.*

*Instead of participating in the party, she just watched and seethed. Clearly, something had gone down that day that left her feeling something very negative, but instead of excusing herself from the party, she sat in anger and was being "the party pooper."*

*And the truth is, in this situation, everyone was being bullshitty. We were all feeling Megan's vibe and ignoring it because that was the socially acceptable thing to do. We've been taught that our emotions are not acceptable, especially to strangers or acquaintances, so no one said a word. Megan*

*had made a choice to show up at this party, punishing Chris,*
*herself, and ultimately all of us. Every time I started to relax*
*or laugh, I would glance over and see Megan's angry stare*
*burning a hole into my soul. She wasn't happy, and she didn't*
*want anyone else to be happy either.*

*When we get stuck in our bullshit, we do not care about*
*if our energy is negatively affecting the room. In fact, we*
*want everyone to notice our bullshit. It's a way to gain atten-*
*tion. It's a way to garner energy from the room. It's a ploy*
*for control.*

---

## GETTING TO NEUTRAL

Emotions aren't logical—literally, they originate on a different side of the brain, remember? No one wants to sound like
the crazy person. We all want our feelings and experiences to
be validated, but if we're stinking up the place with our bad juju,
we need to move the energy. So, if we're having a moment, we
need to express our funk in a nondestructive way. Our emotions
are wonderful because they make us human. We feel the world
around us, and our emotions color our experiences, but when we
let our negative emotions run the show, it's like trying to ride a
tidal wave. In the heat of the moment, we forget that emotions
are fleeting and impermanent.

We've all been there, whether it's a knee-jerk reaction when
we're fighting, not letting go of being "right," that anger that we
carry toward another person for far too long, the fear-based
bullshit you can't let go of—there are a million ways this manifests.
A lot of times, when we get into these extreme places, we can get
stuck in our story, which acts as a feedback loop that just makes

our bad vibe worse. You'll know you're in a loop when you start thinking in superlatives: *They* never *do this* or *They* always *do that.*

One tool that we use is a time-out. When you're feeling overwhelmed, emotional, or out for blood, take time out to get grounded. In the moment, it can be really challenging, but giving yourself a little room to breathe is key. Once you've gotten some space, pay attention to how you're feeling—angry, sad, whatever—and just give yourself a moment.

Once you're calm, take a moment to see if you can look under your initial emotional reaction. Maybe you're resentful because you're feeling abandoned that your friend bailed on your plans, or maybe you're not feeling witnessed, or you're feeling out of control, or maybe you just have low blood sugar and need to eat. Our emotions, especially strong ones, are important. It's our body sending us feedback—so pay attention. Once you've gotten to the root of your reaction, give yourself some space to have compassion for yourself—we don't practice this enough. We're human beings trying our best, and it's messy. There is no way around it.

## HOW WILL YOU SHOW UP?

For a simple way to call yourself or another person out on bullshit, ask yourself this question: What's motivating me right now? If the answer is that you're motivated to control, hurt, or punish another human being or yourself, you're being a bullshitter. If you're secretly motivated to gain approval at all costs, or willing to cut throats to get ahead, you're a bullshitter. If you're not even willing to answer the question of what motivates you, because it just seems too real of a question, or you don't like the answer, well, then you're definitely a bullshitter.

On some level, we're all absolutely full of shit. We say we're confused when we don't want to take responsibility for ourselves or our mistakes. We claim innocence when we're thoughtless. We deny our bad behavior, instigate fights, and then act like we have no idea why everyone around us is so upset. Sometimes creating bullshit feels good. It feels like we're part of something. We get hooked on the drama of our own messes and fall in love with our story.

Unaddressed bullshit will get in the way of everything. The cycle goes something like this: You feel overwhelmed because you bit off more than you could chew at your job. You become overwhelmed and start a fight with your friend or family member as a way to discharge energy. You use said fight as a great excuse to not get your work done. You show up at work and lie to your boss. You've had a terrible weekend! You weren't able to complete the project because—because—well, because your dog died! Or your grandma. Or both. They both died in a car accident over the weekend. Then you feel offended that your boss doesn't seem sympathetic enough about your fake deaths.

That is a bullshit cycle at play. Now, when did this cycle start? When you weren't honest with yourself about feeling overwhelmed or limited.

Once bullshit is called, it's impossible to ignore. It's putting your finger on exactly what the stinky smell is. Once you name it, you can't pretend you don't know what it is anymore. Ask yourself what to do with the bullshit. Trust yourself to answer the question.

Now the question becomes, not *if* you're being a bullshitter at times, but instead, how willing are you to call bullshit when you feel it? Learning how to call bullshit will save time, energy, money, and ultimately your happiness. If bullshit is running your life, chances are there is very little room for anything else. The first step is to acknowledge your choices and actions. Don't fall into a hole of shame because you've noticed you're being bullshitty. We're all guilty! And we're all powerful enough to change. Remember: *you are not your bullshit*. The upside to seeing and calling bullshit is that once you know it's there, you can work to clear it.

It's amazing how so many people are willing to deny their own happiness to stay in a stinking pile of shit because it seems more comfortable than just naming what's really going on under the surface. We see our peers bullshitting themselves into lives they hate. Taking crappy jobs or making bad decisions because they listened to their parents, their teachers, or their friends instead of their own hearts.

Maybe if you stopped letting your bullshit run your life, you'd accomplish something magnificent. Or maybe you'd try something new. Perhaps it's just easier to keep things exactly as they are. If you don't try for anything too big, you won't get hurt. Right? This is obviously the three-cans-of-whoop-ass portion of this book. We call bullshit on one another. We know that human beings are flawed. Bullshit is *always* present. The question is: How willing are you to let it run the show?

Anything worth doing takes a degree of courage that seems just a little bit insane. Especially when those dreams or relationships or leaps into the unknown are so outside the box. You deserve to love your life, love yourself, and love what you create. You are designed not as a vessel for your bullshit but actually as a vessel for creativity and light in the world. And heads up! We don't want to be the only ones in our generation being the "hype men," trying to get everyone else excited to be here. We need you to get clear about what you love and what motivates you. We need you to wake up and start living and creating your dreams because we can't course correct this generation alone. We need help. We need your honesty, heart, and desires so that this is a world worth living in.

## HELP YOURSELF

- Acknowledge your bad vibes.

- Express your feelings in a grounded manner that won't cause damage or injury. Holding on to them is like poison and will only cause more harm.

- Get it out. Scream in your car, go for a run, beat up a pillow. Move that energy through your body.

- Remember that you are in control of yourself, your emotions, and your response.

- Accept responsibility for your part. Sometimes we set ourselves up to feel resentful or give away our control.

- Try to understand where the other person is coming from. This can give you a look into their point of view and may give you compassion for their situation.

- Clear it. Clear it with your friend, partner, the universe, in a clean way.

- Take a good, hard look at your own bullshit. How can you make some changes to show up to the world less bullshitty?

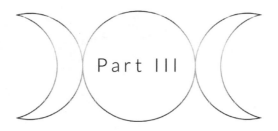

Part III

# BE YOU,
# BOO

# CHAPTER 8

# DO YOUR OWN THING

## THE APPROVAL VORTEX

When we rely on our intuition, our feeling body, and our authentic self to navigate the world, we step away from what we think we *should* be doing—to what simply feels for now. It's the most liberating and wonderful decision you can make, but it's not always easy. As we've discussed, too often we look to others to find out what we are "supposed" to be doing, and it can be a vortex.

Growing up, we all go to elementary school, high school, some go to college, some finish, some don't. Since we grow up in these incubators, we are all "on the same page" to one extent or another. But once we're dropped off into adulthood without a map or directions, it's easy to still want to look to those same friends or peers as indicators of success. On the other hand, when we throw away the map of where we should be and go our own way, we step into life. We're happy because we're in alignment with ourselves.

No matter what choices you make in your life, someone is going to have an opinion about them. The problem with playing to the approval of others is that their endorsement of a false self isn't ever going to feel good. Having another person's approval of you isn't going to fill in the gaps. It's the very reason that so many people freak out once they hit middle age. They've built their lives valuing the opinions of others over their own authenticity until the tension between who they really are and the person they've created becomes too much. So they go buy a Ferrari, or have an affair, or start making choices that seem totally insane to those around them. It's up to us to take the hero's journey inward and start living fearlessly before we've built lives that don't authentically serve us.

When you go your own way, it can be intimidating at first. When you step out of that matrix of validation, people are going to try to put you down. They'll tell you you're crazy; they'll make passive-aggressive comments to make themselves feel better about their choices. Haters are going to hate—but don't pay any attention to them.

When you're walking your own path, a path that perhaps isn't the norm in the world in which you grew up, standing up and claiming your life as your own isn't easy. In fact, we're both being constantly asked to reaffirm our approach in life. We call these moments when we're really reaching, and perhaps even frustrated, taking a seat on the "struggle bus." We've seen how being really *real* can make others very uncomfortable and even angry.

While it's not an uncommon reaction to have people in your life try and hold you back from growth, this is mostly because of how that growth will bring up their own internal fears and limitations. For the most part, when you get pushback from anyone about living your truth, it actually has little to do with you.

That said, we know that just because you're growing and changing doesn't mean you want to abandon the relationships and connections that are most important to you. In fact, our greatest hope for you is that by being more authentic and more real with yourself, you'll be more available to the deep connections that matter most in your life.

Living authentically means that you are connected authentically. Being "real" means that you can grow authentic, deep relationships from the rich gardens of your heart instead of trying to grow a garden in the parched earth of the unhealthy ego.

But there will be struggle. There always is struggle.

## Sonia Steps Out of the Closet

*When you live an intuitive life, a lot of time it means not caring about what people think, trusting your Spirit instead of the noise. But growing up, I was shy and sensitive. I started prekindergarten a year early and was perpetually picked on, which, in turn, made me even more quiet. The last thing I wanted to do was stand out. But when your mom is known as the "psychic" around town, you kinda stand out. Even having grown up in this world, it can still be a struggle for me. When I was a kid, I was always quiet about growing up in an intuitive household. But various friends' parents knew my mom was a "psychic" and would make disparaging remarks or quiz me. Their favorite game: "What am I thinking right now?" or "Tell me something I don't know." It overwhelmed me, so I decided to keep it on the down low. I thought that it was my business, a private part of my life, and I didn't want to explain anymore.*

*I went off to college and was welcomed into a very academic environment where it felt like the world needed to be based in fact. I also didn't want to be the "crazy" intuitive girl, so I kept it quiet. I would fly to teach workshops with my mom, do readings, and counsel by phone, but I never uttered one word about it to my peers. My ego was solely at the helm of this decision—I just assumed people wouldn't get it, but a deeper part of myself was struggling. I wasn't being true to who I was, how I was raised. I felt like a hypocrite—coaching my clients to live an authentic, heart-based life while hiding away a fundamental part of myself for fear of judgment.*

*Finally, my senior year was starting to wind down, the air of uncertainty was palpable, and I felt it. But I had a secret weapon: my intuition. I knew if I followed it, I would be okay. I wanted to help my classmates and friends, remind them that they were smart, wonderful, and that they too had an inner GPS, but I didn't want to "out" myself. I discussed the dilemma with my mom, and she simply said, "Just be who you are." That was enough. I finally thought,* Fuck it. Who cares what they think and whether or not they get it? This is who I am. *I started with my friends, who welcomed me with open arms; they loved me no matter what. I started to talk about it more and more, to everyone and anyone. To my surprise, most people "got it." What a shame my ego had kept my gifts closeted this whole time.*

*Of course, I encountered people who wanted to argue with me, prove me wrong, tell me I was crazy, but my mom's words rang in my ear. I was given a huge gift in learning that I don't have to "explain myself."*

---

Shakespeare said it best: "To thine own self be true." When we live from our hearts and live full out, we don't ask others for permission or approval. It's a different energy, not one that is adversarial, but rather in knowing ourselves and what we need. When you live an intuitive life, you take full responsibility for your actions. It's empowering. We play full out, live life to the edges, learn from our mistakes, and lead with an open heart—we see the goodness in life, in ourselves.

Our mom would constantly tell us to "mind our business." She knew, being a successful spiritual teacher, that there were people out there who thought we were downright evil for teaching others to trust in the power of their own gut. But she always reminded us that the hate of others wasn't our business. "You can't control how other people perceive you. You can connect to your own heart and live your life from that place." She's spot-on. It wastes time and energy to overly concern ourselves with how other people perceive us. Instead, ask yourself, *How do I feel about me? Am I proud of my courage? Am I being honest despite the haters?*

In our family, we often say to one another, "Do you, boo boo. Do you." This is code for *Listen to yourself and take care.* So we'll say it to you now. When you're getting pushback from your friends or family, or if perhaps you've just taken a seat on the struggle bus and are having a difficult time changing your life, remember: Do you. Do you, boo boo.

## I DECIDE

To live a truly spirited life is to live a life of conscious decision-making. Too often, people are willing to abandon themselves, their needs, and their desires to the whims of others because they don't want to make a choice. But in life, there is always a choice. By not making a choice you're making a choice.

You're a powerful being by definition. You create your own experience whether you are consciously doing so or not. Each moment is a creation, so your challenge is to create something that feels good *for you.* If, on the other hand, you don't take the time to get to know your authentic self and Spirit, it can become very easy to confuse what you want with what others want. If you go unconscious, you may find yourself in all sorts of situations where you allow yourself to believe this is "good enough" or this is "bearable" even though you're miserable.

Here's a little secret we can let you in on: deep down, most people don't really give a shit about what you're doing or not doing. Truly! Most people aren't that concerned with others at all. We've spent countless hours counseling people. We know what people are concerned with—themselves. And this isn't a bad thing! In fact, we encourage our clients to invest less in the thoughts of others and focus instead on themselves. When we raise our own awareness and listen to ourselves, that's when our lives can really open up and transform from mediocre to magical.

We were at a party in Chicago one night at the house of a friend who works in the music industry. A semipopular DJ was playing. He seemed like a nice guy, but something about the vibe was off. He is in his mid-30s, and while we were chatting with him, his girlfriend, who was barely 20, approached us. She was gorgeous, fashionable, but a little standoffish and looking very unhappy. We mingled with some other friends, leaving the two in the corner. Later that week, a good friend scoffed, "That guy, he can be really nice, but he cheats on his girlfriend all the time. Last time I was at a show with him, he blatantly hit on me while his girlfriend said nothing. He's kind of a creep. She's only with him because he's famous. It's really sad, actually."

It was such an interesting moment because it became clear she probably wasn't happy in her relationship but stayed in it for the "perks." People do these things a lot—staying in a job, in a relationship, in situations that don't serve them, because of what others may think. But in those quiet moments, when we tune in, we know better. Guidance tends to arrive in those moments where we can finally admit to ourselves, *I'm unhappy.*

If we're not tuned in, we abandon ourselves for what we *think* we want. People don't like to make decisions because they don't want to be responsible for the outcome. But the white knight we are waiting for is our authentic self—the one who decides.

### The Best Worst Boyfriend

*Cheryl, a successful celebrity stylist, called me after cheating on her boyfriend of four years. She was absolutely distraught. She had never considered herself the type to cheat, let alone with a young model she met on a video shoot. She sobbed that ugly sort of cry when describing how terrible she felt for betraying her "sweet" and "innocent" boyfriend.*

*Despite her own emotional upset, I could feel that Cheryl hadn't cheated on her boyfriend because she was a deceptive and manipulative person. Instead, it felt like there was more to the story, and with a little digging we could get to the bottom of what was really happening.*

*I asked about her boyfriend, Joe. He was a successful lawyer and, at 30, was well on his way to a high-powered position at his law firm. He drove a beautiful car, lived in a beautiful home, took her to gourmet meals, and treated her very well. He looked the part. Her parents loved him. Her dog loved him. Everyone loved Joe.*

*Something within their relationship must have created enough tension for Cheryl to cheat.*

*"All right, Cheryl. I have a question." I paused and waited for her to acknowledge that it was okay for me to proceed. "What quality attracted you to the man you cheated on Joe with? I'll assume he was good-looking, since he was a male model, but what else? You're around gorgeous people all the time. So what was it that felt so attractive?"*

*She reflected for a moment as she wiped her nose with her sleeve. "He talked to me."*

*"What do you mean by 'talked' to you?" I nudged.*

*"There was a dog on set with us that day. The photographer had a puppy. It looked exactly like the dog I had growing up." She cleared her throat. "And Dominick, the model, noticed that I really liked the puppy and I started to tell him about my dog growing up. And I opened up to him. One conversation led into another. I told him all about my family. I told him about my dad's alcoholism and my mom being crazy. I told him about growing up in the country and moving to Los Angeles with no money. I told him about wanting to move back to the country one day and open a small organic farm. Dominick asked questions. He felt interested in more than just the simple answers I give most people."*

Cheryl's reason for cheating had nothing to do with sex. What Dominick did was pull her into her authentic self when he showed real interest in her. And as she began to open up to him, she connected to her heart. She connected to her dreams and yearnings, and that felt good. It felt good to share herself with another human being, but it mostly felt good to connect to herself.

*"How about Joe? Do you talk about these things?" I asked.*

*"Yes and no. Most of the time when we go out, I do all of the talking. He's quiet. He doesn't always ask follow-up questions. I don't think I've ever even told him I wanted a farm."*

So despite how Joe read on paper, all was not working for Cheryl on the inside. Their connection, despite her logical mind telling her that he was all she ever wanted, was lacking a quality of authenticity. Joe was ideal, but he wasn't deep enough for Cheryl. Instead, Cheryl was constantly trying to get Joe to open up himself. She felt isolated in her own relationship and didn't even realize it.

*Cheryl had built a life around how her boyfriend looked to others instead of how he felt to her. She was in a relationship with a great guy, but wasn't feeling connected to him authentically. She cheated on him when she genuinely connected to another human being and was her authentic self. That's why the affair had little to do with sex. Instead, it had everything to do with being a deep-sea diver person in a shallow pool of water.*

## DO NOT DRINK THE KOOL-AID (EVEN IF PEOPLE TELL YOU IT'S ORGANIC)

Like lemurs, many people follow the group and jump right off the cliff with a glance at their neighbor and a "What are we doing?" while plunging into the abyss. When you're not tuned in to your intuition, life turns out like that a lot. You end up at the bottom of the cliff, all broken and bruised, wondering how the hell you got there.

A study, called the Bystander Apathy Experiment, conducted by John Darley and Bibb Latané back in the '60s, used college students to highlight the dangers of groupthink. The experiment was set up like this: The subject knew that they were going to participate in a psychological study. The subject was led to a waiting room with others, who were also going participate. They were given clipboards with forms to fill out while they waited for the experiment to start. Unbeknownst to the original subject, it already had. While the other participants filled out their forms, the scientists started to fill the waiting area with smoke, simulating a fire in the other room. The other "participants" continued to fill out their paperwork as if nothing were wrong. The subject of the experiment was timed to see how long it would take them before they notified someone about the "fire."

Some people waited 20 to 30 minutes to notify someone about the imminent danger in the other room. Some people said nothing at all. They waited to take cues from their neighbors. On the video, the subject looks up in alarm, waiting to see if anyone else would react. Some people just burrow their heads down into their paperwork. Some people panic, waiting for affirmation from neighbors. How insane is that? You would assume that if your life were in danger, you would say something. But that is the overwhelming power of groupthink. It will overtake you and leave you vulnerable if you don't stand your own ground.

With intuition, you learn to notify people of the "fire" that you feel. People may look at you as if you are crazy or overreacting. This is a way to make themselves feel comfortable. When you learn to tap into your intuition, you have to do this all the time. And we won't kid you—it can be extraordinarily difficult. There are many times when we have ignored our intuition in order to make others more comfortable. But after so many of these "would have, could have, should have" moments, isn't it wiser to yell, "Fire!" instead of pretending that the smoky waiting room is exactly where you want to be?

The most interesting thing about groupthink is the sentiment that if you're not with us, then you are against us. There is no space for anything else. It's very black and white. But you can self-select out of that dichotomy and create a third space of what is good for you. Life is not one-size-fits-all, so things that work for your friends, co-workers, and partners may work for them but not necessarily for you. Instead of spending that energy trying to make it work, spend it by doing what works *for you*.

## DON'T HALF-ASS; ALWAYS USE YOUR FULL ASS

In order for this book to be at all effective, you have to be willing to do something different. Being willing to play full out means throwing yourself wholeheartedly into something. It means actually following through and showing up for yourself. The reason to show up full out and play is because it will open doors for a new experience. The definition of insanity is doing the same thing over and over again and expecting a different result. So what we are suggesting is to just try something different. You can always go back to your old ways. Believe me, the old hat will still be there if you put it down and try on a new one for a while.

We tell our clients to protect their dreams and their hearts like solid football linebackers. Don't fall into the trap of thinking that just because you want to be authentic and honest, everyone else is going to keep up with you. Instead, be compassionate that they're where they need to be, and you're on your way to something new.

We've seen how damaging it can be when those in your life do not witness you accurately. And we know the pain you might carry in your heart for not feeling witnessed by those you love. But nothing is quite like being willing to grow up and see yourself for the gorgeous and unique person you truly are. And if you're just solidly on the struggle bus in this department and can't find your own inner self-confident cheerleader, fake it until you make it. Decide that you're going to say nice, encouraging things to yourself. Write yourself notes and leave them to find around your house. They can say things like, *You're doing an awesome job. Or, I love you! Keep going!* It might seem cheesy, but those small encouraging notes, even from yourself, will remind you to keep putting one foot in front of the other.

When you know yourself, know your Spirit, you know who you are. The power of that is immeasurable: you don't take shit, you don't have to ask for permission, you don't live your life to please others but instead follow your own compass. You can look your own fears in the face, take a breath, feel it, and still be guided to what is right for you for now.

Your life is happening *right now*. There is no enchanted potion, nothing is going to magically fall into place, and life is not going to be great one day unless you make it great. Remember who you are, remember what you love, remember that you are incredible, remind yourself that you're not stuck and you can make your dreams happen.

## HELP YOURSELF

- Catch yourself when you're self-conscious by asking yourself if you're being too concerned with the thoughts of others.

- Trust your gut.

- Write encouraging notes and leave them around your house to find.

- Put a reminder on your phone that pops up and says, "You're gorgeous and I love you. Go for it."

- If you feel groupthink overtaking you, excuse yourself and reassess.

- Don't ask for opinions. Seriously. It doesn't matter. No one gets to decide for you what's going to work for you.

# CHAPTER 9

# I LOVE ME
# SO MUCH

## I LOVE MYSELF

We have been conditioned to believe that doing things for ourselves first is selfish and self-absorbed. We have all had the experience from back in kindergarten when we wanted to play with a toy but the teacher would intervene, reminding us to "not be selfish." We would begrudgingly hand it over and wait for our turn. When we're little, it's an important lesson to learn. But we're adults now, and we don't always have to hand over our toy just to be "nice." When being "nice" is the goal, we usually abandon ourselves and our needs in order to not make others uncomfortable. We're basically being total a-holes to ourselves. We need to unlearn taking care of everyone else's needs before our own.

Here's a secret: if we don't act in a self-loving way, we're going to resent the people that we're being "nice" to. So we have to learn to be nicer to ourselves, and that starts by becoming curious about what we need and then doing it first.

When we take the time to check in with ourselves and our desires and take responsibility for them, it's not selfish, it's self-loving. Self-love is the most important trait we can culti-vate—how much love and respect we have for ourselves dictates what kind of partners we'll choose, how we see ourselves, and how we carry ourselves in life. As RuPaul says: "If you can't love yourself, how the hell you gonna love somebody else? Can I get an amen?"

Amen, Ru. A-MEN.

So, this self-love thing? If you're new to the party, here are some of the basics, you gorgeous bright light.

## ROW YOUR OWN BOAT

Try out this new motto: "Me first." After all, we are the only experts on how we feel, what we need, and what we want, and, at the end of the day, we are solely responsible for making it happen. We need to be responsible enough to row our own damn boat. That means no stowaways we secretly hope we will inspire with our buff rowing arms and who will finally decide to help us row. (Who doesn't love a toned upper bod?) It can be scary because there might be the fear that we will leave people we love behind. But being self-loving isn't abandonment or dumping someone in the middle of a lake with no life vest; it's an awareness and responsibility for our well-being, our happiness, and making that shit happen. We're like cars: we need to fill up our tank of gas, otherwise we'll end up stranded on the side of the road.

The paradigm we've all learned is if we take care of everyone else's needs, they will magically return the favor. It doesn't work like that. And it really doesn't work like that if you don't know what it is you need or where your boundaries are. Then you're just playing with fire and everyone is going to get burned. Maybe you have seen this in your own life. If we look at our resentments, more often than not they are tied to taking care of others' needs while abandoning our own, i.e., overgiving, not knowing when to say no, or not being real about how we feel with people in our lives.

Imagine you have a roommate who is supermessy, but you don't want to say anything because you don't want to cause a fight. Not self-loving. Call that lady out, but in a way that's loving and respectful: "Nicki, it makes me feel bad and think that you don't respect me when you leave your dirty dishes all over our apartment, especially since we've already had this conversation before."

Being self-aware, taking responsibility for our lives and ourselves, is the most self-loving thing we can do. Remember: "The general drinks from the well first." Drink up. When we come from a place where we are well cared for, we can show up to our relationships from a place where we have something to give.

Currently, if you're giving to those in your life from a sense that you *should* or you have to give to be a "good person," it's like being powered by a battery instead of plugging into an outlet: you'll deplete yourself completely and end up angry, resentful, and stretched too thin. Giving from obligation instead of a real heart space will only lead to anger and resentment, so first things first. Give yourself some space. Give yourself the kindness, consideration, care, and compassion that you want from others and ultimately want to give to others. If you give yourself first what you deeply yearn for, you'll be a lot happier to give back to others in your life.

---

## Sabrina Chooses Self-Love

*My entire life I have been what some have called a very high-maintenance person. I was born into this world with food allergies, sleep issues, and anxiety attacks. I have a learning disability that made it so I had to constantly have extra help and attention from my parents and my teachers. I always needed what felt like more than my peers to just get by in life.*

*These needs are not only extremely specific but, frankly, a pain in the ass to fulfill. The upside of this constant neediness is that it cultivated an extremely powerful tool for me, especially when it came to my health and education. I learned early on that in order for me to get my needs met, I had to know what they were and be willing to speak up about it. Any negative or shy energy I had when asking for what I needed would just create confusion.*

*One evening, my ex-boyfriend and I had a series of misunderstandings and miscommunications that left us both feeling a little off. I'm someone who needs time alone to recover my energy, especially when it's been less-than-smooth sailing, and he needs to feel connected to get grounded once again. We watched a TV show and headed to bed, where I could feel his needy energy. I felt annoyed. I just wanted to read and be left alone. Usually, we would be in an energetic standoff, me reading and him feeling like I didn't care. This time, though, I rolled over and said, "I just need some alone time to recover. I'm not going to go away. What do you need?" He then told me that he just needed a moment to feel connected in order to feel safe and like we had genuinely cleared the air.*

*It was so simple: once I was able to ask for what I needed in a grounded way and allow myself to take care of me, I was able to be genuinely available to what he needed with a generosity of spirit where I wasn't annoyed. This shift had a profound impact. Being aware of what my needs were and their importance allowed me to have compassion for myself— which allowed me to have compassion for him as well.*

*When I am connected to my heart, I want to love and champion those around me. When I am in my head and convinced there just isn't enough of whatever I want or need to go around, there's a voice in me that wants to shove people out of my way. Have you ever seen those horrifying Black Friday scenes of people trampling one another to get the best deal on a television or microwave? Remember how I felt that day I wanted to curse Santa Claus among all the happy holiday shoppers? When we truly believe we're not going to get what we need, human beings have the capacity to trample their own grandmothers.*

*Sometimes, we just have to be the one to get our needs met for ourselves. Knowing what we need, and then taking action to give it to ourselves, sets us up to be happy people. It means that we can give to others in our lives because we're clear about what we need first.*

---

## HIGH FIVES FOR EVERYONE

What we're asking you to do is change your perspective that self-care isn't selfish but self-loving. When you do things to take care of yourself, you fill a deep well. We've all been there: when you have given too much, stretched yourself too far in helping others—and then snapped. Because when you give and give, you expect others to do the same, and when they don't, you become angry and resentful. You might even take some pride in your martyrdom—"Look at how special I am because I give so much!" This is an ego trap. The ego comes and reminds you how special you are—no one is as good as you! Ugh, what B.S.

But if we take care of ourselves, fill our own wells, we become better receivers and givers. We hear our intuition, our boundaries, and our needs clearly. We give from a place of wholehearted generosity. The great thing about this overflow is that we can show up for the people we love with a happy heart. We don't come from that begrudging place. We spread the love around. If you've ever had a really good day and just feel like sunshine, you want to spread that magic to everyone around you. High fives for everyone!

We can start small, giving ourselves that love, compassion, and care that we need. Then we can show up to our relationships, our work, and our community, grateful to be able to contribute. It ripples out. It's simple: if you want to feel good and open your heart, first be good to yourself and then be good to others. No martyrs allowed.

---

## PHOEBE FORGETS SHE'S NOT A SAINT

*I had a client named Phoebe who called me bedridden and sick. She was a sensitive, empathic, creative young woman who lived in San Francisco. Although she was only 29, she had spent her life giving and giving to those around her, and, unfortunately for her, her body rebelled against this overgiving. She developed a series of autoimmune disorders that basically left her needing to be alone in bed for days on end.*

*Before she got sick, she would spend her time care taking and managing the people in her life. She would offer to do anything and everything for those around her, but would regularly forget to even feed herself. She gave her ex-boyfriend her savings when he racked up parking tickets. He never paid* her back. She volunteered to lead every work project; she was the shoulder you could cry on if you needed her; she was there to pick you up at the airport no matter the weather, or the time, or what she had to do that day for herself. Her entire identity was centered around selflessly giving to those around her, despite what she needed.

"And now I'm alone," she told me. "I am sitting here, totally in surrender to my body, which is just no longer willing to go along with my agenda. And, truthfully, when I really look back at all those 'overdoing it' experiences in my life, it was constantly coming from a place of wanting to be worthy of love or to prove to everyone around me that I was good. There were times that I so wanted to say no, to take care of myself, but I just felt like people would get angry. I was so scared that they would be upset with me for saying no, so instead I always said yes. And now I can't even get out of bed. I know what got me here—my own stubborn nature. Because the thing that's so interesting is that for all of those times I was so there for everyone else, when I really needed them, most of my friends were nowhere to be found."

Phoebe and I worked to heal her life by starting with her own heart. Instead of pumping energy into everyone else, it was time for her to get centered on what it was that she wanted for herself. To get Phoebe moving again, we implemented a "self-check-in" system. She started with a 20-minute daily morning meditation. Before she got out of bed, it was important that she took the time to check in with herself, and to know her own needs before addressing anyone else's.

Then, she would take out her journal and write herself a list of five things she needed to accomplish that day. Getting out of bed, making her bed, taking a shower, going to the grocery store, and doing the laundry was a simple typical list *in the beginning. This exercise acknowledged her own needs and allowed her to focus her energies on herself. Accomplishing the list made even the smallest of tasks feel like a success. She began to see that she really could put herself first.*

*The next piece was learning to ask those around her for help. This meant that Phoebe would pick up the phone and ask her friends and family specifically for what she needed that she was unable to do for herself. She'd call her brother and ask him to take her to her doctor's appointments, or call her friends for help with errands.*

*Slowly but surely, identifying her own needs became easier. Now that she knew how to ask, Phoebe even found that those around her were open and receptive to helping her. As she started to heal, she realized that the real problems were her own lack of boundaries and self-love that kept getting in her way. Before jumping in to rescue others, before offering to fix something that wasn't her problem or be the solution to someone else's plight, she would pause to consider the offer first.*

*She called me one day, sounding triumphant. "Last week a friend wanted to attend a work conference out of state for a weekend. She has three kids, no extra money, and no babysitter. I could feel my urge to offer to watch her kids while she was away. Instead, I took a deep breath and just listened to her. I hung up without offering to be the unpaid babysitter, and she called me yesterday to say her sister would come in for the week to watch them. The kids were ecstatic to see their aunt, and the whole thing had worked itself out without me being the solution."*

## LEARNING TO MAKE SWEET, SWEET LOVE TO YOURSELF

Learning to love yourself properly, and fully, is a skill that they should teach us as a mandatory life requirement—like learning how to read.

We have seen it over and over again: the extent that we love ourselves is directly connected to the amount that we can enjoy our lives. When we are cheap with ourselves, when we are withholding or cold, when we put ourselves down and beat ourselves up for being human, we limit the quality of our lives. We know the power in a self-loving routine because, like good oral hygiene, we need to maintain our self-love schedules. The more consistent you are with self-love, with saying self-loving things and treating yourself with kindness, the easier and more natural the process will be.

You have to start by honestly assessing how loving you are currently being to yourself in your life. Do you stop to check in with yourself regularly, if at all? Do you make choices that honor your heart? Do you pay attention to the negative thoughts and criticisms that your brain rattles off?

Many of us have a constant stream of self-analysis and critical self-talk on play every day. Our thoughts are powerful. They affect us deeply. We both have a powerful affirmation practice of self-love and leave little notes around the house for ourselves to find, like a loving Easter-egg hunt. (*You are beautiful inside and out!* pops up on my phone once a day.) We long to have other people say wonderful things to us, like "You are important" and "You matter," but we have to be willing to say these things to ourselves first. It's amazing how powerful these affirmations of love and honoring can be.

At first you may have serious reservations, or might feel downright silly with all the "rah-rah" cheesiness of it. But give it a try. You might discover that you flourish with positive, self-loving statements. We know we do. And the more we can say them, and the more we can correct the negative, self-hating affirmations with positive self-loving ones, the better life feels.

Here is a list of some examples of positive, self-loving affirmations:

- I love you so much.

- I am so loved and lovable.

- My presence is important.

- I am grateful for my beautiful heart and beautiful life.

- I love myself fully.

Repeat these affirmations, once in the morning and once at night. Your ego will judge and say that it doesn't matter, that saying nice things will do nothing, but over time, and with consistency, you will begin to naturally gravitate toward a gentler and more loving inner dialogue.

We too have struggled with self-critical and self-hating talk. It's easy, at every turn, to find something wrong with ourselves. We judge our bodies, comparing them to the images we see on Instagram and in fashion magazines. We too have been guilty of comparing ourselves to those around us and ultimately coming out feeling less than, unlovable, or unworthy. So learning to talk sweetly to ourselves, learning to disengage and call out the bully who lives in all of us, is our work in the world. We know the power in changing the inner dialogue because we have committed ourselves to being safe and loving people for ourselves and for each other.

The model of Jesus on the cross, the martyr, or the saintly holy person who is willing to die for everyone else's needs, is an ideology that is ultimately killing us if we don't break the cycle. We're not Jesus, we can't walk on water, so let's stop expecting ourselves to do so. Instead, by becoming self-loving, self-centered, and connected to our own hearts *first*, we can be available and present. What's amazing is that giving from this place of wakefulness to your own heart means what you give doesn't deplete you and leave you feeling empty, dead on the inside, and hating everyone around you. Instead, the natural urge to give can spring forth and nourish you as much as those you're touching, helping, or healing.

## RECHARGE YOUR BOD-ERY

Now that we've covered some of the basics of self-love, let's get into self-care. All that loving yourself is awesome, but you need to put it into practice. If you are aware and loving to yourself, then self-care follows suit. Self-love and self-care are the best things for your Spirit, your intuition, your happiness, and your well-being. In fact, self-care is the most direct way to express self-love. Self-care is being aware of what you need and then doing it, without drama. Tired and don't want to go to the party? Call your homie and bail. Feeling anxious and overwhelmed? Go for a walk, or call a friend who will listen to you vent.

Self-care includes taking care of your body, feeding it things that make it happy, and moving. Or if you've been working nonstop, self-care can be letting your hair down, going dancing, and not being *so* responsible for a moment. The most magical thing about self-care is that a little goes a long way. The more in tune you get with yourself and your Spirit, the easier and easier it becomes take care of it.

If you're really struggling, start by asking yourself these questions:

- Did I get enough sleep?
- Do I need to eat and/or drink water?
- Do I need to move?

- How do I feel?

- What do I need?

- What is the last thing I did that was fun?

- What was the last thing I did where I was in the moment?

These are clues to things we love and need. When it comes to self-love and self-care, our job is to be attentive, loving, and endlessly interested in what we need, and do it without guilt. So, go on, grab yourself a bouquet of gorgeous flowers, take a hot bath, treat yourself to a massage, or have a dance party for one in your living room because you love yourself.

## HELP YOURSELF

- Create a routine of self-care—meditation, exercise, eating right, getting enough sleep.

- If you're in a situation where you are caretaking someone, ask yourself, "What do I want to do?" Bring it back to yourself.

- Don't say yes when you mean no—aka boundaries! If you're not sure if you want to do something, say, "I'll get back to you," or "Let me think about it."

- You don't need a crisis to justify a break. If you're overextended, go for a walk, get a massage, put yourself in time-out, write in your journal, go hang out with your friends—and do it guilt-free.

- Make a habit of checking in with yourself. It's easy to go on autopilot and forget to check in with how you feel.

- Remove yourself from situations or people who are damaging to your Spirit without having to explain yourself. Be protective of your self-care and your Spirit.

# CHAPTER 10

# BE A
# GIVER

## THE HEART IS A GIVER

What this book is inviting you to do is break with your social conditioning and connect to your heart as the true captain of your ship. This reorientation will shift you out of constantly over-analyzing and critiquing yourself and will allow you to be present in the moment. This journey from head to heart will open up your life to miraculous movement forward and will deepen your experience in the here and now.

The by-product of this shift is marked by one key signature. The heart, when it is awake and in play, wants to contribute. When we break out of the story that there isn't enough, or that we aren't enough, and move back to our purest self, we want to add beauty to the world—sharing our gifts, talents, ideas, conversation, or just good energy.

If we live in our naturally designed way, from our heart center, we're givers. It feels good to give, to show up 100 percent and give without expectation—simply for the joy of it. If you've ever hung out with little kids, you know they are always trying to help. They just want to contribute, whether it's helping push the grocery cart or clean up. When we live from our hearts, we connect to the joy of life, to our generosity of Spirit, and to one another. Rather than looking at one another from the paradigm of "me against you," we find similarities rather than differences and see it as "me *and* you."

In our society, and especially as women, we're encouraged to give selflessly, and at the same time we're taught that no matter what it is we want—goodness or money or love—there just isn't enough of it to go around. This incredibly draining belief is a lie. We had a very successful screenwriter friend who was constantly worried that there wasn't going to be enough money, enough time, or enough of the world to go around. She was preoccupied with "getting hers," or what she felt she was owed, and interestingly enough, she was constantly having that reflected back to her with shitty experiences of lack. Her house was broken into. She lost all of her luggage on a trip to India. Friends would unexpectedly drift out of her life or betray her. But what is important to recognize is that her focus and intention was on seeing life in this way.

The truth is that when we connect to our hearts, or to a source bigger than ourselves, we realize how vast our capacity to give, and to receive, really is. The world is truly abundant. We move out of being fearful and shift into helping and uplifting each other.

We're naturally designed to be open-hearted and giving. We come in with our hearts wide open. In fact, science shows that charitable giving lights up the dopamine reward pathway in our brains. It feels good to give! And the wonderful thing is that it is just a breath away. When we open up our hearts and are generous, we get out of our own heads and start to see how we can contribute to the world. It's the shift between a taking energy and a giving energy. When people are generous of heart and spirit, it's a reward unto itself. Giving with an open heart from a well-fed space, without expecting anything in return, no strings attached (not even that secret one!) makes you feel like you get to sprinkle happy dust on everyone around you. It inspires people to do the same.

## WHAT DO YOU LOVE?

The spirit of giving can absolutely infect you. Let it. Consider what happens around the holiday season every year. We feel this magical energy—the spirit of giving. It's tangible and real. The spirit of the season has its own vibration. Be open to the possibility that the spirit of giving can become the flavor of your life.

The simplest way to start giving is to do what you love and follow that path. If you're unsure, think about it. We love helping people connect back to themselves, to their intuition, and back to their heart space. Every day we pinch ourselves that we get to be cheerleaders in people's lives. Being generous doesn't have to mean huge gestures that take up a lot of time or money. It doesn't have to be a big deal. You can be generous with your time by simply asking someone, "How are you?" in a genuine way. One of the most important, often overlooked, ways we can give back to those in our lives is by truly listening to people when they speak. Can you recall the last time you had a really deep conversation with your best friend, where they just were able to hear and see you, or you hear and see them, without judgment? If so, what a gift! What a gift to be able to listen to or feel heard by a loved one.

If we follow our hearts and share the things we love, it comes easily. You can feel it. The question is, what do you love? The possibilities are endless. Love cooking? Cook a meal for your friends or family. Donate your time at a soup kitchen or do meal prep at a shelter. Love animals? Head to the local animal shelter and volunteer to play with them or take them for a walk. Pick up garbage in your neighborhood. Throw some protein bars in your car and give them out to homeless people. Buy a new pack of white tees or underwear when you're at Target and give them to your local shelter. It can be as simple as just asking someone if they need help. The sky is the limit. When you do what you love, giving comes with ease.

## JAGGER SAID IT BEST: "YOU GET WHAT YOU NEED"

So you wanna be a giver? There's a catch: you have to do it with no strings attached. That means no secret, back-pocket agenda that if you give, then people need to give back to you. When we give to get, it's not really giving. If you think like that, you set yourself up for one of the easiest pitfalls: resentment. Resentment is the worst because it creeps up on you. So here are the ground rules for giving.

Check in with your boundaries. We're talking about all-out giving, doing it because it feels good and it opens the heart (and lights up the brain).

When we show up with no strings attached, we open ourselves up to a whole world of abundance. We open our hearts and tune ourselves in to start to see generosity and receive it ourselves. When we are generous and trust that there is enough in the universe, we get back our investment tenfold. Being generous of spirit allows for energy to flow. When we are stingy, the world becomes stingy with us. Sometimes it's hard to trust, and our egos are on patrol. They whisper: *Be on alert! It's not safe and you'll get ripped off.* But being authentically generous is always a good idea. It'll surprise you with its goodness.

Often, we are looking to fill some sort of void—whether we're trying to find happiness, find self-worth, or even just feel better. Most of the time we look to all sorts of things to fill that void— whether it's buying stuff, numbing out with TV, drinking, getting high, any form of social media. The list is endless. But that hole we're trying to fill won't go away until we decide that we want to shift something.

But when you shift your attention onto others in a genuine way, you can finally get out of your own ego, where nothing will ever be enough, and into your heart space, where there is more than enough. It's pure abundance. Take a moment and think about the last time you did something nice for someone, something that made you feel good. It could have been as small as a phone call, an encouraging comment. The frontal cortex of your brain lights up and makes you want to do more good things. Start doing little things for the people around you; pay attention to how it makes you *feel*. Call your grandparents or send a postcard to a friend and start to get high on giving. It'll feel better than anything you can buy.

---

## Sonia's Favorite Flower

*The other day, I was all in a tizzy about the million and one things I wanted to accomplish. I am learning astrology, so I wanted to study, finish my "fun" book, make dinner, call my family, and refill a prescription. To top it all off, I was supposed to go out to breakfast with my sister and her friend. I woke up stressed out. I just kept adding to the never-ending laundry list in my head. And I was being incredibly hard on myself. My ego kept telling me:* You're so lazy. I cannot believe that you're waiting until today to do all these things. It's never going to happen, buddy.

*So I "read" for more than a half hour until Sabrina asked me what I was reading. I had absolutely no idea as my mind was obsessing about all of the other things I needed to do. When she pulled me out of my spiral, I knew that I needed to get grounded and present in my body. So I went outside and worked out. I ran until I felt like my legs were going to give out. I channeled all that nervous energy into my body. I literally ran away from the fear and anxiety until I didn't feel it anymore. When I stopped running, I paused, took a deep breath, and felt so much better.*

*I could feel the sun on my back. I smelled the flowers, the fresh air. I could feel the blood circulating through my veins and my lungs expanding and contracting while catching my breath. At that moment, I looked up to see a woman tending her garden. She was holding a bird-of-paradise flower whose stalk had been trampled by a previous passerby. She clipped the bent flower, looked at me all sweaty and red-faced, and handed me the flower. "Here's for a job well done," she said, and went back to tending her garden. I was surprised by the gesture. I managed to stammer out a "Thank you," but she was so deeply involved in her flowers, present in her moment, that I don't think she heard me.*

*The woman gave me a gift from the universe. As I trotted my sore butt back home, I wondered what to do with my new flower. I twirled it around in my hands and examined its structure and beauty. I admired how it looked like an actual bird, with its long, thick petals that looked like a beak, and its "wings." I approached my sister's apartment and saw a man burrowed into his iPhone with a scowl on his face, walking his large black lab. I knew exactly what I should do. I walked up to him stood directly in his path and just said, "This is for you." He was stunned. I didn't wait to see his reaction. I just walked into my sister's apartment complex and, in my gut, I knew that he'd needed a gift at that moment.*

## GRATEFUL FEELS GREAT

What are you most grateful for right now? What makes you bubble over with contentment when you bring that person, place, thing, or feeling into your awareness? Is it your pet? Your bed? Your best friend? Your gorgeous Spirit? Your significant other? Your cute butt or your fierce hair?

Are you grateful for your talents? Your struggles that have shown you your depth? Your teachers? Your soul's willingness to learn something new? Your creative potential or artistic abilities? The breakfast you ate or the delicious fruit at the market down the street?

The trick here is that when you get stuck in a vibration of lack, allow yourself to bring gratitude into your heart. Feeling like there just isn't enough in the world to go around will make it nearly impossible to trust enough to let go and give back. So focusing on what you're already grateful for in real time and space means you can contribute from your heart, and not just your fears or ego. Real gratitude will jump-start your car back on the road toward being able to contribute to the world from a place of connected-ness, instead of just sheer willpower or a belief that you *should* want to give no matter what you're going through.

The thing is, being giving doesn't just mean that you have to physically GIVE something. Sometimes, just offering a little room to breathe and shifting the perspective from judgment to com-passion is an enormous way of giving back.

No matter what we're feeling, if we start to look at what we're grateful for—even if it's a shitty experience—we can change our perspective from being a victim to being responsible and back to our hearts. When we connect to our feelings and our heart space and come from a place of gratitude, giving comes easily. It allows us to have compassion for ourselves and others.

## Sonia and the Flash

*Right before I left for college in Portland, Oregon, one of my best friends died. When I started school, I opted to spend a lot of my time alone. I would ride the "Raz," the school's bus that dropped us off downtown, and wander around, listening to podcasts and taking photos. Portland has a large homeless population, but it didn't bother me. Having grown up in Chicago, I was accustomed to people from all walks of life, and I knew that most of these people either suffered from various forms of mental illness, struggled with drug addiction, or rode the trains up and down the West Coast.*

*One sunny afternoon, I was sitting by a fountain taking photos when a homeless man approached me. Earbuds in, I offered a halfhearted wave, but the man wasn't going anywhere. I pulled out my earbuds and turned to him. He introduced himself as "Flash Gordon" and pulled up his sleeves to display his biceps, one tattooed with the word Flash and the other Gordon. We started chatting. He was kind, telling me about how he'd wound up homeless on the streets of Portland. Interested, I asked Flash, "What would you do if you could do anything?"*

*His face lit up. "I have always wanted to be a singer/songwriter. I am self-taught, but I love singing and playing. It's my dream to be famous." I loved his enthusiasm and excitement.*

*He then asked, "Would you mind taking my picture? I don't have any recent photos of myself." I obliged, and Flash started posing, showing off his tattoos, flexing, and having fun. I joked, "This is for your new album cover, Flash. You look great." After our impromptu shoot, he wrote down the address of the homeless shelter where he was staying on a receipt I fished out of my pocket. Figuring this was the end of our interaction, I told him I would drop off the photos sometime the following week.*

*Flash started walking away but then turned around and shouted back to me, "Sonia, I want to show you something." The idea of following a homeless man to a second location made me hesitate, but my gut told me to go. I put away my camera and followed a few paces behind Flash until we arrived in front of a bar. Being underage, I hesitated. What in the world were we doing here? Flash saw the look of unease on my face but gestured for me to enter. Inside, I followed him down to the basement of the bar, where there was an old, janky piano. Flash sat down, cracked his knuckles. "This is the song that's going to make me famous—I've been working on this for a little over a year." He started playing.*

*Now, in a movie, Flash would have been a prodigy, but this was real life. He was awful, but he played with his whole heart and soul. The moment he played the final chord of the song, the bartender walked downstairs and shooed us out.*

*We emerged back into the daylight, Flash beaming with pride. It was time to catch the bus back to school, but not before Flash walked over to a flower box, picked a tulip, handed it to me, said, "Thank you for treating me like a human," and walked off. When I boarded the bus back to school, I sat and looked at that flower and knew that Flash had given me an enormous gift. I was so grateful that I'd been able to witness his generous spirit. After spending time with him, I suddenly became aware of how grateful I was for my life. He changed me that afternoon—he was fearless in sharing his gifts, his stories, and his life with me. And he showed me such humble gratitude in just paying attention and listening wholeheartedly. I no longer underestimate what a few minutes of time, along with genuine interest, can do.*

*After my afternoon with Flash Gordon, I realized that although I was still in deep grief, I was ready to start seeing the goodness in life again. That evening, instead of retreating to my dorm to spend the weekend alone, I decided to reach out to some girls who had been trying to befriend me since arriving at school. These girls are my best friends to this very day, and I am grateful to Flash for giving me the courage to be uncomfortable and reach out.*

---

Being grateful is a highly self-loving choice. When you can see all the flowers in your garden and your heart is filled, you want to share it with everyone. You want to brighten someone else's day. Each individual affects the whole, so when we choose to be in gratitude, everything opens up. When things aren't going our way, we often take a moment and think about everything we are grateful for. Sometimes it feels hard, like shifting out of that lower vibration is betraying how we're feeling, but once we start noticing the good things—even if it's just a cup of morning coffee— and as we cultivate that habit, our list starts to grow.

Learning to be grateful is another way to train your mind to be aware. Most of our lives, we're on autopilot, and we don't even notice what we are grateful for. We're trained to pay attention to what's not working—what went wrong during our day or who did what, and we forget to focus on all the great things that surround us. Like nurturing any new habit, at first it might be hard—your mind might go blank or you might feel like you need to "reach" for the things you're grateful for. But if you start to take moments to appreciate things you genuinely love, you become filled from the inside out.

## COME SIT WITH US

We can tell you from experience that living an authentic, heart-centered, intuitive life is pretty awesome. Of course, everyone will experience some bumps in the road, but that's life. We're inviting you to live a life that is blessed with grace, abundance, and joy that emanate from within. With these tools, you can change not only your world but you can also become a light for others around you. We're inviting you to shift out of fight, flight, and freeze mode and move into the flow where you ride the wave and trust yourself. Where you can listen to your intuition, your gut, and your heart as your compass, get happy and spread that shit around.

There's a lot of noise and fear in the world, but when you live a heart-centered life, you know that there's nothing to be scared of. There is no *them*; there is just us. As Gandhi said, "Be the change you want to see in the world."

When you slow down a little bit, get present, and connect, you feel the magic and joy of life—no matter what is going on. You become responsible for yourself, for your life, for your own happiness, and become a beacon for others—a gift. The great thing about living from your heart is that you inspire people to do the same. Just by being yourself and showing up, you raise the energy and the bar. You want to change the world? Do it by showing up, being present, sharing your gifts with the world—using your voice and being loving. It's simple but revolutionary.

What the heart intends to create, it does. So if your intention is to look for the good, to expect good things, and to allow for goodness in the world when it does arrive, you can bet that your life will have some pep in its step. If, on the other hand, your intention is to experience struggle and secretly hope that the world will prove you wrong, well, it won't. Your experience of the world will always follow your own internal intention and focus. So we invite you to let your life be spiritually invigorated by generosity and openheartedness, because above all, the whole world loves the lover.

Life never stops, and it's an illusion that someday we'll get to a place where we'll magically be given permission to relax and enjoy its gifts. So instead, slow down and connect to your heart, enjoy the ride of life instead of focusing on the destination. Be a believer. Be a giver. See goodness in yourself and others. Choose to be your brightest self by realizing that you're already an amazing person, just as you are *right now.*

## HELP YOURSELF

- Value your gifts and share them with others with no strings attached. Cook a dinner party for friends, volunteer in your neighborhood, register people to vote.

- Give a shit! When we care and show up, we can create huge shifts in the world.

- Pay attention and exercise gratitude every day, even if it's just for your cup of coffee. Watch your list grow.

- Nurture what you love and encourage people to do the same—you're a bright light in the world, and when you shine, you help others do the same.

- Take a minute and smell the flowers. Be grateful. Life isn't a destination; if we pause and enjoy, we can stop fighting against life and start enjoying it.

- Tell yourself all the things you love about yourself, as you are right now.

# ACKNOWLEDGMENTS

We would like to acknowledge all the awesome people who helped us create our book, beginning with our mommy. How can we ever begin to thank you? You are our heart, and we are so grateful to you for teaching us to believe in ourselves, to listen and trust our intuition, and to follow our Spirit. You've always shown us we can do anything. You are an amazing role model; thank you for always having our back, being our believing eyes, and always supporting us, no matter what. We are so grateful to have you as our mommy. We love you more than anything in the world. Thank you to our dad for always holding down the fort, gathering us at the dinner table every night, and teaching us to be badass women. We love you.

Thank you to our devoted editors, Alexia Paul and Sally Mason. Thank you both so much for helping shape our voice into the clear message that it has become. Your patience, encouragement, and skilled editing have polished our message in so many needed ways, and we couldn't have created this book without you.

We would also like to acknowledge our fabulous publisher, Reid Tracy at Hay House, who has known us since we were teenagers and was so willing to be our publisher. Thank you, Reid, for seeing us, and for championing our message. Thank you also to Patty Gift for believing in us and giving us the chance to share our message with the world, and for all the wonderful people behind the scenes at Hay House who have helped bring this book into being. We are so grateful to all of you for all of your fabulous help and incredible talent.

Thank you, dear Rebecca Campbell, our beautiful soul sister and friend, for your practical and heartfelt guidance in helping us get grounded and clear in all the ways in which we could shine even brighter. We bow to you in gratitude. And to Jenny Johnson, for your creativity, devotion, assistance, and continued support along the way. Thank you for being there and being so helpful in our confusion. We are so grateful to be able to depend on you in so many ways.

Thank you to Rena Trindl, for being such an advocate and helping us bring this book into the world. Thank you to Colin Ofloy, aka Crocodiles Out Late, for your incredible work and helping us when we were in panic mode over our book cover. Thank you to our sister, Simonne Solitro, for being our cheerleader, our best friend, and our favorite playmate. We love you so much. Thank you to all of our friends and family members (who we would love to name individually, but that would probably take a lot of space), who have loved and supported us over the years. We are so grateful for your friendship and you mean the world to us. You guys are the real MVPs. And finally, thank you to every single one of our readers and new BFFs.

# ABOUT THE AUTHORS

Sonia and Sabrina Choquette-Tully are sisters and best friends who Skype daily and Snapchat often. Babies of a true self-help mama but also children of the '90s, they understand the pressures facing their generation and have taught workshops focusing on intuition, Spirit, and creating a ridiculously magical life. Website: soniaandsabrina.com

We hope you enjoyed this Hay House book. If you'd like to receive our online catalog featuring additional information on Hay House books and products, or if you'd like to find out more about the Hay Foundation, please contact:

Hay House, Inc., P.O. Box 5100, Carlsbad, CA 92018-5100
(760) 431-7695 or (800) 654-5126
(760) 431-6948 (fax) or (800) 650-5115 (fax)
www.hayhouse.com® • www.hayfoundation.org

**Published and distributed in Australia by:**
Hay House Australia Pty. Ltd., 18/36 Ralph St., Alexandria NSW 2015
*Phone:* 612-9669-4299 • *Fax:* 612-9669-4144 • www.hayhouse.com.au

**Published and distributed in the United Kingdom by:**
Hay House UK, Ltd., Astley House, 33 Notting Hill Gate, London W11 3JQ
*Phone:* 44-20-3675-2450 • *Fax:* 44-20-3675-2451 • www.hayhouse.co.uk

**Published and distributed in the Republic of South Africa by:**
Hay House SA (Pty), Ltd., P.O. Box 990, Witkoppen 2068 •
info@hayhouse.co.za • www.hayhouse.co.za

**Published in India by:** Hay House Publishers India,
Muskaan Complex, Plot No. 3, B-2, Vasant Kunj, New Delhi 110 070
*Phone:* 91-11-4176-1620 • *Fax:* 91-11-4176-1630 • www.hayhouse.co.in

**Distributed in Canada by:**
Raincoast Books, 2440 Viking Way, Richmond, B.C. V6V 1N2
*Phone:* 1-800-663-5714 • *Fax:* 1-800-565-3770 • www.raincoast.com

Take Your Soul on a Vacation

Visit www.HealYourLife.com® to regroup, recharge, and reconnect with your own magnificence. Featuring blogs, mind-body-spirit news, and life-changing wisdom from Louise Hay and friends.

Visit www.HealYourLife.com today!

# Free e-newsletters
## from Hay House, the Ultimate Resource for Inspiration

**Be the first to know about Hay House's dollar deals, free downloads, special offers, affirmation cards, giveaways, contests, and more!**

 Get exclusive excerpts from our latest releases and videos from *Hay House Present Moments*.

 Enjoy uplifting personal stories, how-to articles, and healing advice, along with videos and empowering quotes, within *Heal Your Life*.

 Have an inspirational story to tell and a passion for writing? Sharpen your writing skills with insider tips from *Your Writing Life*.

## Sign Up Now!

*Get inspired, educate yourself, get a complimentary gift, and share the wisdom!*

**http://www.hayhouse.com/newsletters.php**

**Visit www.hayhouse.com to sign up today!**

 HAY HOUSE

HAYHOUSE RADIO
*radio for your soul*

 HealYourLife.com ♥